THE DEATH AND RESURRECTION OF THE EPISCOPAL CHURCH

HOW TO SAVE A CHURCH IN DECLINE

Caswell Cooke Jr

ISBN 978-1-64569-638-4 (paperback)
ISBN 978-1-64569-639-1 (digital)

Christian Faith Publishing, Inc.
832 Park Avenue
Meadville, PA 16335
www.christianfaithpublishing.com

Printed in the United States of America

For Janice!

Enjoy!

[signature]

Sept '22

This book is dedicated to

Christine, my wife;
Leah, Maddy, and Louie, my children;
Margaret Phelps Speer, my grandma;
Patricia A. Healy, my mom;
Everett L. Perrin;
George E. Kent;
The Rt. Rev. David B. Joslin;
The Rev. Robert W. Anthony;
And to all of my church family at Christ Episcopal Church
in Westerly, RI, a place you should all come visit!

This book is a tool for growth. It is not based in scripture; it is not spiritual in nature. The book does not attempt to interpret the Bible or use it to justify anything contained herein. It is practical, blunt, and brutally honest. It is written out of love for the Episcopal Church and mainline Protestant churches in America. It may offend some of our members, but it is worth the read! Hopefully, it challenges you to make a difference.

Prologue

A couple of years ago I was having a conversation with an Episcopal priest. I was lamenting how our parish, over a decade ago, had to sell our rectory because we couldn't afford to keep it. I was also saying that if trends continue, someday we will have to sell our parish hall and continue to further reduce our footprint.

What I was expecting was for her to say that we need to work hard to get people into the church and help them understand why supporting the work of our parish is so important to our community.

Instead, the response was "What are you afraid of?" She said that no matter what happened, the faith community, which is Christ Church in Westerly, Rhode Island, would always exist somehow.

And that is my problem with what's going on in the Episcopal Church. I understand that God works in mysterious ways, and I understand that not all institutions are able to be preserved or saved. But I do not want to just *exist somehow*.

I, for one, am not going to sit back and watch that happen, and then twenty years from now stand by as my church gets sold or closed down. I don't want my church to simply exist one hundred years from now as some long-lost scholarship fund or whatever vestiges may be left after the building is sold and the cross is melted down for its weight in gold. I don't need Christ Church to be a performing arts center or a cool-looking restaurant.

My thought is, shouldn't the church strive to be the center of activity in our communities? Wouldn't it be easier if we had a place that we could afford to maintain and staff that we could afford to keep on the payroll so that we didn't have to worry about those issues and instead could focus on the needs of the community? We would be free to work on issues, such as people who are homeless, people who need help paying the rent, people whose children have special needs, and so on. We could perform better outreach if we were not always worried about paying the electric bill.

In order for the church to help the wider community and the wider world, we need to have our own house in order. If we dwindle to the point of nonexistence, we will then switch to being strictly in survival mode (as many parishes already are) and we will no longer be able to harness the resources and the numbers to go out and help the community and start wonderful programs that benefit where we live.

No, I believe it's time to turn our focus to preserving the institution which is our Episcopal Church. And I know that runs contrary to what a lot of people think, but I, for one, don't want to continue to watch 35–50,000 people leave every year. At that rate, in less than twenty years, we will be gone. We have lost half of our membership steadily in fifty years, and a quarter of our membership in the last decade alone.

No one is sounding the alarm for the Episcopal Church or other mainline denominations like the Lutherans, Congregationalists, Presbyterians, or Methodists, so I will. If you care, read on!

CHAPTER 1

We Have Arrived at the Fork in the Road

I've been a member of the Episcopal Church since I was born. I guess that makes me a *cradle Episcopalian*. My baptism happened forty-four years ago, so it's been quite a while and I have been proud to grow up and be a part of Christ Church Westerly in the Diocese of Rhode Island.

When I was eight, I became an acolyte and also joined the choir at my church and sang all through my formative years. I can remember singing multiple services on holidays, as well as being an acolyte at one service on a Sunday morning, followed by singing in the choir for the next service. I always loved the church and was fascinated by it growing up. I love the ceremony and the pageantry and the music.

Most importantly, I love the family that my church still is all these many years later. It is probably the only constant in my life. Growing up I had two great role models: one was our rector, Robert W. Anthony, and the other was our organist and choirmaster (who recently celebrated his sixtieth anniversary as such), George E. Kent. They taught me so much and greatly influenced my life.

I attended Roman Catholic school from first grade through twelfth grade, so I also had another religious upbringing and was able to distinctly see the differences between the two faiths. I have explored other religions and other denominations of Christianity. I have been to many great cathedrals from, Westminster Abbey to the Washington National Cathedral, to St. John the Divine and to churches from Boston to New York to Florida.

Things changed a little bit when I went to college and was in my twenties. While I maintained an interest in the church and attended infrequently at Trinity Church in Copley Square, Boston, it wasn't until I hit thirty that I came back fully. I have two young daughters that attend worship regularly, as well as Sunday school. My wife and stepson, both of whom are Roman Catholic, attend our church more frequently than their own. I chair the communications committee at my church and have served on the vestry for the last couple of years and now as junior warden of our parish. I have also been a delegate to the diocesan convention more than once.

But enough about me, what about our church?

I firmly believe the first thing that all of us have to acknowledge (and by all of us I mean the faithful at each parish which includes the leadership and the clergy and those who attend on a regular basis and have a stake in the church that they belong to) is that our denomination, like many other denominations across our country, is declining. In fact, I would say it is spiraling toward its demise on its current trajectory.

While I feel that the current presiding bishop Michael Curry is a breath of fresh air and has a wonderful message with the *Jesus movement* and his message of *love* so beautifully amplified at the 2018 royal wedding in England and that the bishop of my diocese in Rhode Island is the best bishop we have ever had and is the person we need to lead us at this time, the message of the national Episcopal Church fails to resonate with most parishes, especially in rural and suburban areas.

Our national church is very right to point out racial inequality in our country and promote reconciliation. I am very proud that our church ordains women, marries people that are LGBTQ, and ordains people that are gay or from any other walk of life. We don't judge, and we are truly an open church. I am a dad who was not married when my kids were born. Somewhere else, that might be a problem. The Episcopal Church does not shun me for who I am.

But let's face it, the everyday life of a parish in suburban Wisconsin or Maine or Ohio doesn't focus on these issues each day of the week. Nor should the national church only focus on social justice issues and forget about the people they already have in the pews or, in the current case, had in the pews.

There is more than just reconciliation that needs to be talked about. I think it's time that what we talk about is surviving as a denomination because we do so much good for this world. And, honestly, we could do even more work if we had greater numbers. But if the church declines to nothing, we won't be able to do much at all. Our collective voice will only be a faint whisper.

Every year, when we lose another thirty or forty or 50,000 members from our denomination, the usual talking points come out. We changed how we count numbers back in the nineties, we don't have as many children as we did back in the sixties, or churches that used to be in a once populated or affluent area—well, all the people moved out of town and no one is left.

Dr. Kirk Hadaway, until his retirement spent over a decade as Episcopal officer for congregational research, wrote extensively on church and denominational growth. I always look at his analysis and insight. When I read his interpretation of the decline, he makes it not sound so gloomy. But in reality, it is. We have not *bottomed out,* as the Rev. Ian Markham (Virginia Theological Seminary) preached back in 2013; we are in a downward freefall.

We can make excuses and we can point to other denominations that are also dying. The Lutherans, Methodists, and the Presbyterians are in a very similar boat as we are. But that is not going to turn around our collective problem. If our message is narrowcast and our national church is trying desperately to appeal to only a few segments of our population, then few will hear it. In twenty years (or less), many of our parishes may just be well endowed museums with caretakers and the ones that have no endowment will be sold off for spare parts.

But there is something that gives me hope. According to the last census, there were anywhere from three to three and a half million people in the United States that identify themselves as Episcopalians.

Yet our membership rolls show us somewhere around 1.7 million and shrinking rapidly.

At our peak in 1966, our denomination had 3.6 million members and has been in decline ever since. It's a decline that has never reversed. It did slow in the 1990s, but over the past decade has accelerated to the point where we have lost 25 percent of our membership since 2004.

So it seemed to me that the first thing we should do as a denomination is turn to those other one and a half million people that already identify themselves as Episcopalian and invite them back to our church. Or how about the 750,000 expat Brits or British Commonwealth that live in America now? Many of them will have had a history similar to ours since we are part of the Anglican Communion. Those folks are ripe for a message from our Church because most of them are familiar with it. This is the low-hanging fruit. Pick it!

You've noticed it, and I've noticed it. Dozens of people that we knew growing up who still live in our towns, cities, and communities just don't come to church anymore, and I bet none of them ever received a phone call or an e-mail or a letter simply saying, "We miss you" or asking why. So many of the kids that grew up going to Sunday school and are now in their twenties and thirties are gone and we don't follow up. So when they have children themselves, their kids don't get any of the same upbringing.

I'm going to lay out to you what I think our church needs to do on the national level, on the diocesan level, and on the parish level. Let's put it this way, nothing else that has come down from presiding bishops or bishops or priests or committees has worked since 1967 when our denomination began to decline. Yes, there are a couple of dioceses that are bright spots. Yes, there are examples of churches or cathedrals that have turned it around. Yes, there are places where being really liberal or really conservative have worked. Yes, there are successful alternative worship experiences or services in Spanish or Chinese. But that is the minority, not the majority, of what is happening. And these bright spots are not enough to reverse the decline alone. When I hear that average Sunday attendance across this nation is less than sixty, I realize that there are very few more years that we can survive with just those numbers. And those numbers keep going down.

In fact, every initiative or declaration or change in policy or change in prayer book or change in liturgy has usually, mostly, caused people to exit. Sometimes when we preach to people who are not a part of our denomination, it actually offends the people within our own denomination that are already here and supporting our church. I know there are conservative and liberal elements in our church and both of them think we are losing members because we are too liberal or too conservative. I say we need to take a deep breath and relax.

And even though I'm not a priest—I'm just a simple layperson—I'm going to be straight up and honest with the leadership of our church. This book is for all those in authority in our church, including priests, deacons, bishops, wardens, vestry members, committee members, ushers, and delegates to diocesan and national convention, executive committee, as well as all those who want to see our church thrive and prosper and grow. It's even for our presiding bishop to read if he has time. In fact, I am available if he wants to hire me.

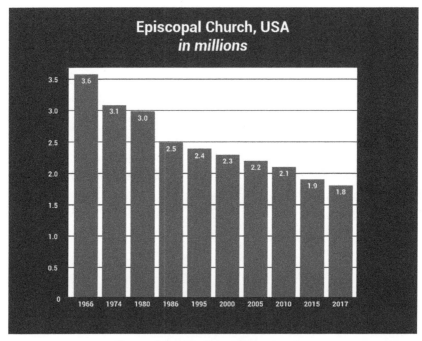

Chart of the Decline of Membership
1966–2018

CHAPTER 2

Reality Check: Having Your Clergy, Vestry, and Faithful Core of Parishioners Face Reality

Listen, I think it's great that the presiding bishop gets on a plane to go to different parts of the world to proclaim the gospel. It's okay that he goes to Ghana to apologize for slavery. I don't criticize it, although I would not make it a priority if I were in charge.

I think the first priority should be educating all of the clergy, as well as vestry members of each parish, on the fact that we used to have 7,500 churches in our country and now we have about 6,500. It's a huge decline in the last twenty years. That's over 1,000 houses of worship that just simply folded up and were sold off or mothballed. Some of those people find another congregation within the Episcopal Church, some of them find a home in another denomination, and many of them go nowhere. So I think we don't have time to go to Ghana until our own house is in order.

At your next annual meeting I want you all to do the same thing. Show the church's national statistics over the past forty or fifty years. Show them the downward trend. Then look through your parish annual reports and go back as far as you can, showing numbers of pledging units and parishioners and Sunday school attendance. I bet you it matches the national trend. If it doesn't, you are in a bright spot, and I want to know your secret!

What you need to do is have a come to Jesus moment with your parish. You don't need to do this at a Sunday service where visitors or folks that may be on the periphery of parish life are. You need to do this at your annual meeting when your clergy and your vestry and committee members and your most faithful and engaged parishioners are in attendance. Or call for a second annual meeting if it's midyear.

Here is what you do not want to do. When asked about the decline in the Presbyterian Church a few years ago, the Rev. Gradye Parsons said he saw hope in the numbers since the overall decline was smaller than in previous years. "Yes, the numbers reflect a decrease in active members in the denominations… But the numbers also illustrate fewer losses than the previous year." So in the case of that church, he was encouraged that they *only* lost 89,000 that year compared to 102,000 the year before. Come on, people, let's get real. And the Episcopal Church does the same thing. It is time to stop that.

I guarantee you when you show the numbers to your parish most of them will not believe it at first and it may upset them. But after they've had time to think about it, you can then begin to refocus their energy. What does this church need to do to keep its doors open and keep its mission in your town or city? This is a question that the national church cannot answer for you and probably not your diocese, either. Only your church members and leadership can answer the questions.

If you take the next five years to concentrate 75 percent of your energy on growing your church, then you will accomplish it. Five years is all you need to have a success story. And let's face it, in five years if we don't do this, another thousand churches or more are going to close.

There were plenty of years when we had time to form study committees and subcommittees and have a discussion or put off until the next convention what to do. We had that time back in the seventies or eighties. We even had time in the nineties. We can't anymore. It is too late to study the issue. A parish with less than forty pledging units is dead in the next three years unless they have a huge endowment.

The national leadership is not going to be able to help each and every parish across this nation. In fact, when general convention meets, it just seems like there's a lot of discussion about gender neutral language in our prayer book or what other controversial political quagmire we can get ourselves into so that we offend much of our own membership while trying to make some point.

No, my friends, the change has to come from the local level. If you are reading this book, then that means you care enough about your church in your city or town and you can save it. And if your parish is doing well, then you can save the one in the next town over by helping or *adopting* them. We have plenty of mission work to do in our own backyard, in our own diocese. The National Church needs to quiet down, back off, and support. We don't need pie in the sky; we need to get down to brass tacks.

Sometimes this is easier said than done. At my own church I have tried to sound the alarm for many years. First, about a decade ago, we had to sell our rectory because we couldn't afford to maintain it. Around that same time, we could not afford a second clergy member so we were down to one clergy person at a church that always had two clergy and even a deacon. It's funny that during the decline many of our parishioners could not see it, and if they could see, there was no call from the clergy or vestry to actually do anything about it. When I would bring it up, leadership would get mad at me.

So your story may be similar. You may think back a decade ago or two decades ago at the amount of people you had pledging and the number of programs you had at your church and now you don't have as many. You may notice the building needing a lot of work and there's no way to do regular maintenance because of lack of income. You may be down to one clergy person or you may even be sharing clergy with another parish or mission. Your place of worship may have been downgraded from parish to mission status. Perhaps you and another church in the area merged together. That happens a lot. Or maybe if you're reading this your old church may have been shuttered. It's funny even when we get to this place many of us don't wake up and hear the call.

Here is what I would like us to stop doing. I'd like us to stop saying every time we close a church or merge two churches that this is some kind of a *gift from God* and that we are now called to do something different in his service. Honestly, that's BS, and losing churches and closing churches is not a good thing. We need to stop thinking it's a good thing or some kind of new opportunity. We are not *pruning the tree for better growth*. At this point, there is nothing left to prune. We are down to the stump.

It's great to go out to the street and preach and have *ashes to go* and *church beyond the walls*. But let's face it, if we had our way in a perfect world, we would also have a beautiful building, or at least an adequate building, that we are able to afford to maintain and staff so that we can, in addition to surviving as a parish, reach out into the community and do even greater works for children, for the elderly, for those who are abused, and for those who are poor.

If we start from a place of strength, then we can help the rest of the world. If we're worried about our leaky roof, then there's not much we can do for anybody else. And then churches turn inward, and then they die. Some say sell the church and get out of the building. But, honestly, who wants to have it come to that? No, we need to shore up our own foundation first so we can better help the community.

This may take you not one annual meeting but two. You may have to really work hard on your clergy and your vestry throughout the course of the year to get them to decide that the main focus is going to be on growth.

And then let me put it to you another way. If these folks won't listen, then it's time to change your vestry. You need people who are going to focus on the numbers and attendance and have a definitive goal year after year until you reach a level at which you are confident your church can survive for decades to come.

You've got to make it clear to your parish that they have to stop any and all bickering amongst them. Any kind of cliques in your church or infighting, you need to get those people together to suspend those arguments for a couple of years. Sometimes people feel the choir has too much power in the church or that the altar guild is dictating too much or that the Sunday school is suffering because the rector doesn't feel youth ministries are important. You need to tell them it's time to *suck it up, buttercup* and put those petty differences aside or on hold at least for a few years so that you can all concentrate on one thing and one thing only—growth in membership.

If one of the vestry people or the clergy in your church will not bring up the numbers, then you need to stand up and do it yourself. Go into your church office and pull the records and get it done. Stand up. We have a democracy in this church. Have your voice heard. You may have to do this more than once, and you may have to invite yourself to a vestry meeting and do it three months in a row. But eventually they're going to understand that there is a systemic problem and it's called bleeding numbers.

Remember to get the statistics for the last forty or fifty years or at least the last twenty. That way the current rector won't think you are picking on him or her. As I said, a lot of times, what the current rector will do is show you the membership trend of the last two or three years and how one year might be better than the year before by about 1 percent and everybody feels great. But when compared to twenty years ago, it's still dismal, so you need the long view to compare yourself now to where you have been in the past.

The other thing you need to understand is that there is no one coming to save your church from on high. The national church and even the diocese can't do what you yourself and your fellow parishioners can do for your own parish. Each and every parish needs to take responsibility for what they're doing, and they must turn it around and grow or face death as an organization.

There's one other thing that I think is important to bring up. All too often when we are told that we need to go out and get people to come to our church, we are also told that we're going to need to change how we do things. That we're going to have to stop playing the organ and pick up a guitar instead. That we're going to have to modernize the language or change which rite we use. That we're going to have to stop using incense because somebody may sneeze or that we're going to have to be something different. I'm tired of being told that, aren't you? Also, given the numbers and lack of success, it clearly does not work to change for the sake of change. The only thing it does is drive out the few faithful people we have left. So let's do ourselves a favor and ignore that advice that we've been given for the last generation. Thank you for your attempt, national church, but, no, thank you. Renaming Sunday school and calling it Christian formation won't grow the program, it will just make people scratch their heads.

No, the answer is to go with the energy. What is it that you do at your church best that you are most proud of? Answer that question and that will lead to growth. You don't have to change yourself to attract some fantasy parishioner. You need to show off what you do so that others will come in and understand why you are there in the first place.

So how do we get people to come in? If I've got your attention up to this point, then I invite you to read on.

CHAPTER 3

The Basics Are Simple

There are a few first steps. Some of you have already done this, but many of you have not.

So what does that mean? It means go back to basics. The first thing that we have to do is make sure our church has adequate signage, advertising, and physically looks inviting and attractive.

It's also important that entering a church doesn't seem like a foreign thing to a newcomer or a visitor. Signage and translating Episcopal words are important. We don't need to get rid of the words; we just need to explain them.

Let's start with signage. One thing that is a tradition for just about every Episcopal Church across this country is the wonderful *The Episcopal Church Welcomes You* signs that tell you how far you are from the nearest church. What doesn't work is when those signs are rusted and old and have a couple of bullet holes in them. Or when the main road into town changed twenty-five years ago and we never got a sign put up on it.

The first thing I want your church to do is to find out where your signs are and make sure that they are on every major road leading toward your church if you don't. Make sure they are new. It is the first thing you should raise money for and accomplish.

The second thing is an Internet presence. Your church must have a great website, and it must be smartphone-friendly and it must look good and actually have current and up-to-date information. You would be surprised how many churches just don't have that. Someone has to be tasked with keeping the online presence up to date.

You may have a parishioner that can do this for you at no cost and that is great. But I find that the best thing to do is to hire somebody that does it for a living so there is no hemming and hawing or hurt feelings later on when you change it or months and months of back and forth before the thing is actually live. Just make it a priority and hire someone and do it, just as you would hire an electrician to fix a broken outlet. And, believe me, having a bad or no website is a broken outlet, literally.

The next time you have an annual meeting, you need to put that into your budget as a top priority. People *Google* churches. They don't find them any other way unless they stumble upon them or follow the signs as I talked about before.

What needs to be on your website? First and foremost, great photographs and video need to be on your homepage. Present your church in the best light physically and use photos of the congregation that show various age groups or special programs you are known for.

Service times should be front and center, as well as contact information for people to e-mail. Links to your social media have to be there, as well. The rest of your site could be as populated or not as populated as you would like. You need a mission statement, as well as how to join the choir or become a member of the altar guild, etc. Give people enough information so they feel comfortable coming to services or events. Define terms such as narthex, sexton, and slype and other oddities of our Episcopal language.

Be sure there's a place on the homepage where they can click to donate. Remember, a lot of people nowadays would rather use a credit card or a debit card to pay bills. Many people under forty don't even have a checkbook. You need to make it convenient for them to give to you. So make sure you have online giving, if you don't already. Your diocese can definitely help you with which company to go with and how to get it done. It will be slow at first and people argue about the monthly fees. Hold firm and get it done and eventually you will see results. Define the word *stewardship*. It's not a word everyone uses daily.

Social media is a must. Not only having a Facebook and Twitter and Instagram presence (you can do other social media platforms, as well, but those three are the basics), but having things to post are very important.

So what exactly do you post? Well, I have some expertise in this area because in the past I have worked on the campaign of Governor Lincoln Chafee and ran his Facebook page during his brief bid for president in 2016, as well as consulted the current lieutenant governor of Rhode Island in social media. I also run a page for my own business and a beach area business association.

We built our Facebook page for our business association up to 105,000 people as of 2018. In its category of destination, it is number one in the entire state of Rhode Island. We actually have more people following us than follow our capital city of Providence or our flagship city of Newport or our whole state—something I recently pointed out to the governor.

Why am I bragging about this? Because even a simple, fairly computer illiterate person like myself can figure out Facebook and how to use it. It's not something you should be scared of; it's something that you just need to embrace and try with trial and error. I'm not as good on Instagram and Twitter, but I work on them as well.

Back to when and what to post on Facebook. All of the data points to posting three times a day—morning, noon, and night. They say that most excellent time to post is Friday nights at 7:00 p.m. They also are now saying that twelve o'clock noon during the weekday is also a great time. I don't know who *they* are, but oh well.

What works for posting? Beautiful photos and video work the best. If you have a message to get out, post it with a photo. A lot of times I post events on my church page, and so you want to either have a picture of the previous year's events such as a Shrove Tuesday pancake supper or a Christmas pageant or an Easter vigil.

Every picture tells a story and every picture tells a story best. So try to find good photos from the previous year, and if you don't have good photos of your church, start taking them. Use your smartphone; you don't need a camera. Make sure your photos show a vibrant and full church. In other words, if you have two services on Sunday and one has thirty people at it and the other one has 150, obviously, be sure to share the picture with the church looking the most full. Nobody wants to look at a picture of an empty church. It is depressing to see that, so don't show it.

I digress for a moment when I say that on Facebook I see a great presence from Trinity Church Wall Street. It's a wonderful church that I've been to many times. But when they post their noon day service that has about ten worshipers in an empty church, it kind of makes you feel awkward. It's almost better not to show ten people in a church and just focus on the priest giving the sermon. That way, there's no distraction.

Another example was a church that back in the 1990s would film services from the long abandoned choir loft. The church had so few in attendance that you could virtually lay down in the pews. The tripod that the video camera was on had a slant to it. It was so bad it was embarrassing. I don't think anyone would have wanted to go. All they needed to do was straighten out the tripod and level it and zoom in on the first couple of pews and the clergy on the altar. This would have been 180 degrees different in the visual department, and it could have been a tool for advertising and sharing the gospel to a larger audience.

Obviously, the best time to take photos and video would be Easter or Christmas eve or the day of a baptism. Remember, it's about optics, not necessarily spirituality, when we are talking about social media posts.

Next thing I'll say is that video really works. If you have an iPhone and can use iMovie, which is very simple, that is the best way to get messages out. At coffee hour, have one of your parishioners read the announcements from the bulletin and post it on Facebook. You can make it look professional with the program or an app like iMovie because you can fade in and fade out and you can put music in the background and you can adjust volume. You can also put simple graphics at the beginning or the end. There's definitely somebody in each and every congregation across this great country that is waiting to be asked to use their iPhone in church.

The thing about posting videos on Facebook is that the attention span of most people watching them is usually between thirty and sixty seconds. So full-length sermons might be nice to post, but then if it could be chopped up into several segments, it will get even more views and you will have a post for each of the five days of the week just by serving up the sermon.

A very talented person in my home diocese of Rhode Island named Ron Cowie has been working on videos for several churches and has done a great job. Where I tend to simply post events and what has actually happened that day, he is very creative and will make up interesting commercials, so to speak, for different events held at the church.

One of his first videos that caused a little bit of stir was the fact that we have a *nine-ish* service at our church rather than a 9:00 a.m. service because our priest is very friendly and wants to shake everyone's hand, so, therefore, he is late starting the service. I thought it was funny and quirky, and it got thousands of views. A few in the parish felt it was too silly for church. You'll have to decide the mood of your own parish because you certainly don't want to offend people when delving into humor. On the other hand, just do it because you have nothing to lose.

One of the other great videos made was following one of our bell ringers up to the bell chamber and to view the carillon. Tens of thousands of people watched this video. You figure so many people drive by your church every day, but how many of them have been up in the belfry? When you give them a bird's eye view, the video will spread around your community like wildfire.

We are now at a point where we renovated the inside of our bell tower and are about to start a carillon class for interested people in the community who would like to ring the bells. That all happened because of social media. And it can actually turn into a ministry that would attract people to the church.

Use video to find interesting things in your church building or to go out in the community where your church is active. One of the things that I filmed was when the church Sunday school kids raked a neighbor's yard on a Sunday afternoon. It was great to see all those kids working and to see the couple who are not able to get out and rake the lawn themselves be so happy.

23

We filmed it and posted it in a short ninety-second version, and again thousands of people from the community saw how active our church was outside its four walls. This video also serves in following years to get people interested in the event.

I say film everything you possibly can as long as it's edited nicely and is short and sweet and has good audio. You can purchase a microphone for a smartphone very simply for about a hundred bucks. You can also get a tripod for another hundred or less and have a person in your congregation record the sermon each week or even go *live* during the sermon and stream it.

A lot of people ask about paid Facebook posts. They absolutely 100 percent work. Let me explain how I first got involved with using paid Facebook posts years ago. I book a lot of concerts and have a lot of famous or formerly famous people play down in our beach area. In the old days I would've put an ad in our state's newspaper, which is the *Providence Journal,* and our local newspaper and hope that enough people interested in that particular artist or type of music would see the ad and show up. Today I just click on Facebook and select a radius of fifty miles and type in the artist's name and I can see exactly who likes that person and target only them for this event.

So, for instance, if you are having a pancake supper, you might want to see who in your community is interested in pancakes or Mardi Gras or Fat Tuesday and reach out just to those folks who are most likely to attend by spending your five-dollar or ten-dollar post wisely.

That is another thing. You don't need to spend a lot of money, you can just boost your post for five or ten dollars and you're going to reach so many people. Hopefully, they will actually end up following your page in the process, as well.

In reality, one of the good things that each parish has going for it is that it only has a certain radius with which to draw from before you are in the territory of the next episcopal church. So set your radius on social media ads and broadcast to just that area with a boost of your page to get your followers up. Once the person clicks and follows you, they are going to be a part of your extended family and to receive updates on what is going on, and I guarantee you, at some point during the course of the year, something that your church is offering will strike their fancy.

A great example was a children's Halloween party we offer each fall. We promote it on social media and it is well attended. I recall a young mother and her two children showed up. I asked her how she heard about the event and she responded that she *saw it on Facebook*. How many times in your daily life does someone make that reference? "I saw it on Facebook." So if you are not on Facebook, my friends, they ain't going to see it.

When posting an event poster, make sure it looks professional. It is absolutely essential to invest in good graphics for each of the events you have during the course of the year. Whether it is a church supper, a service on Ash Wednesday, Christmas pageant flyer, or any other events taking place in your parish during the year, make the poster look professional. Once you have created your event poster, it should be good every year if you just change the date.

Make sure that your poster includes all the information that people will need that are not necessarily a member of your parish. Basic things like name of church, address, phone, and website of church and social media logos.

I always say to the folks at my parish that we are very good promoting our events, such as the church bazaar, to ourselves. We get five posters put up inside the church building and think that is sufficient. In fact, when I see the posters, it usually doesn't even say where the event is taking place because the posters are only used in that church. That sort of thing has to end quickly. You don't need to preach to the choir.

Get yourself a simple letterhead that has your logo and phone number and e-mail and address and social media logos on it. Use this for everything, including return envelopes. But for what we're talking about now, you need to use this on each of your posters up at the top or down at the bottom as a way to brand your look in your community.

Ask some people in your congregation to put these out around the town or city. So if you are having a spaghetti dinner to benefit the renovation of your Sunday school classrooms, for instance, you're going to need to put these posters up in your local shopping centers, liquor stores (because they usually have a bulletin board), and any other shop window that will allow it.

The next thing to do is to find out what the advertising rates are on your nearest radio station. In my town we are blessed to have a radio station that is just for the news and talk from our town. So having our priest or event chairs on the air to talk about different things going on is a regular thing for us.

We also do paid advertisement on the radio station to let the people in that community know that we exist. No, not every community has its own radio station, but if you make contacts with the nearest radio station and send them press releases about events going on, then sometimes they make their way into the local news. This is true especially on a slow news day. In a big city, this is harder.

Everything you do should be treated as a new story and you should send a press release out about all the goings-on at your church. Not every single Sunday but certainly for special events or dinners or holiday services or special things, such as lessons and carols or an Evensong or Sunday school registration. You would be surprised how many local talk radio stations are in dire need of people to be guests on shows. So find someone that speaks well on the air and is not shy and get them booked to talk about the upcoming dinner theater event at your parish.

Remember, you do not need to get political or have some kind of left-or right-wing slant or social justice stand with your event. Just do the event!

Now that you've got the Internet covered and social media and the local radio station, it's time to talk about newspaper advertising. I was one of those people that said I never wanted to read my paper online. I always bought the newspaper and read it during lunch. But those days are long gone, and a lot fewer people read the actual paper.

However, the average age of a member of our church right now stands at about sixty-six and I would say that at least half the people that age still pick up a newspaper. So I would use the fifty-fifty rule at this point. Fifty percent of your advertising money should go in newspaper ads that are physically in a newspaper, and the rest should go to the online version of your local newspaper.

There are also ways that your local salesperson from your newspaper can get your ad in front of potential parishioners in your town by using target marketing so that ads appear on screen while people are googling for certain products. Everybody else knows what people want and like when they are online, and somehow you see these ads that actually interest you because of the things you have searched for in the past. Well, there's no reason the church shouldn't be doing that because, after all, it's the twenty-first century, so let's do it.

I also can't tell you how much you need signage outside of your own church for events, for your church itself with service times, and for other types of announcements.

Let's face it. We in the Episcopal Church are very lucky that so many of our churches were built in a time where they were located near the center of the town or near the seat of government or near other publicly used buildings or parks. I'm very lucky that my church is located right next to the town hall and across the street from the library and public park. It is actually in the heart of our historic downtown. In our case, the town hall has no parking lot, so they rely on ours. They installed signs in each parking space that said parking for town hall courtesy of Christ Episcopal Church. That is great free advertising. Take advantage of all situations like that when you share a parking lot.

So for those churches fortunate enough to have such great locations, it's time to start using them. When there are town events, your church should be a part of them, if you are situated in the middle of the action. Use your front lawn to advertise your church. I can't say enough about the fact that so many churches don't have their service times and website in large print clearly on a sign near the road. This is imperative. And when you have special events, don't be shy; put a special event banner right out in your front lawn inviting people to that next event. You have the real estate, so use it.

Take a walk around your church from the angles the public sees it. Look from the sidewalk or from driving past it. Is each area of your church clearly identified and user-friendly? Is your parish hall labeled a parish hall? Is there a sign facing your parking lot that says what the name of the church is, and if so, are service times written on it?

Besides the small signs that are by the front door of most church buildings that are not readable from the sidewalk, do you have a large sign on your front lawn not surrounded by a bunch of shrubbery or covered by trees that really shows the name of your parish and the worship times? If you don't have this, that needs to be a top priority. We went over 175 years at my parish without having a sign on the front lawn. That was changed, and now the casual person passing by at least knows the name and denomination of the church. What the beautiful building that thousands of people pass each day should not be a mystery or a secret. It should be plainly written right out front and it should say *All Welcome.*

Communicating with your parishioners is a difficult thing. In the old days we relied on the church bulletin, as well as perhaps a monthly newsletter that was mailed out to the membership. This is no longer enough. We need to be sending e-mails to anyone that has ever signed a guestbook, or has ever been in the past, or is currently a member of your church. We also need to be able to track if these are getting received and if they are getting opened. We also need to be able to send specific messages to specific segments of the church. For instance, parents need to get special notices from Sunday school, choir members need to get notices from the choir director, ECW members need to get special notices about their activities, and so on down the line.

There are two platforms I recommend that you might've heard of. If you are not using Constant Contact or Mailchimp, then stop what you're doing and do it today. You can send professional-looking designed e-mails on a weekly or monthly basis to your parishioners and find out if they are effective and if people are opening them or not.

Every single e-mail you can find should be loaded into the database because the person who receives it always has an option to unsubscribe to the newsletter. Anyone that signs a guest book, take those e-mails and put them in your e-mail list.

If your guest book or pew cards (please tell me you definitely have those pencils ready) do not have a space for people to write their e-mails, then they are about twenty years out-of-date. Everyone needs to get e-mails of every person that comes to the church or sets foot in the church to keep them informed.

A great way to get people to join the mailing list is *text to join* which is inexpensive and can be directly linked to Mailchimp and other services. You simply text a word, like *join*, to a number you list and it brings them right to the page on the website to enter their name and e-mail. It is simple and it works. Try it at your parish.

I think if you do the basic things we talked about in this chapter and form a communications committee to make sure that these things get done, you will have increased attendance within the year.

You need an advertising budget, so get your finance committee to realize that. I know that last year we had five or six special events that we spent money to advertise, and we filled each one—whether it was the celebration of the sixtieth anniversary of our organist, a Halloween party in our parish hall called *Treats and Eats*, our welcome home Sunday in September, or a special Evensong for our first responders. For us, it cost about $750 for each event. To get a banner (I recommend bannersonthecheap.com), do some radio advertising, some newspaper advertising, posters, invitations for the regular mail, and other means. That might be a lot of money for some churches, but you need to spend in order to bring people in. If your parish is in a city, then it's going to cost a lot more.

CHAPTER 4

Go Out and Tell Our Story

Let me tell you what is not going to happen. People are not going to wander into your church all the time and just automatically become a pledging member of your parish. So you can't just sit there and hope that someone's going to appear. Unfortunately, you're going to have to go out and get them.

If you're a cradle Episcopalian like me, evangelism is not really a word that we use on a regular basis. The Episcopal Church nationally even had a *decade of evangelism* in the 1990s that was met with a lukewarm reception. Many of us are just not the type of people who wear our religion on our sleeve or feel comfortable talking about it in settings outside of the church.

I get it; it's not easy. We have kind of an unwritten saying that says, "You are always welcome to our church, and if you like it, please stay, and if you don't, there's the door because there's plenty of other churches around the town."

We also don't do the guilt thing, so none of our parishioners grew up feeling like they had to attend. We don't have that *Catholic guilt*. We don't preach fire and brimstone from our pulpit, usually, so people aren't afraid and forced to come to our church for fear of going to hell. I'm not casting dispersions on other denominations but I am saying we are not very good at proselytizing and many others definitely are.

We also don't say we are the only way to God. A lot of these other faiths who believe that they are the only way to salvation have that conviction. I don't think we need it because how funny would it be if we thought that the Episcopal Church was the only way to get to heaven? I think even Jesus would laugh at that. What makes us strong is that we acknowledge that we are one of the many ways that lead us to faith in God through Jesus Christ.

But when you stop and think about all of the things that so many parishes around our country actually are participating in, we *do* know how to do evangelism. We just don't know how to connect the dots for the people receiving the benefit of what they get from us.

How many of our parishes run soup kitchens or at least take turns supporting one in our communities? How many parishes do projects in the community like raking a lawn, or rebuilding somebody's porch, or hosting a Thanksgiving dinner? How many have outreach programs to minister to the sick, or shut-ins, or other marginalized groups in our own communities? So many of our congregations already do this work!

So now it's time to showcase that, not only to our own parish but to the town or city in which we live. Whenever we do things to help people as a community we need to document it so that others can see and be inspired to join us in doing.

This is why you must refer back to the previous chapter and be sure to have good photographs and video from every event and function that your church participates in. Promoting what you do online or through a press release to the local media is evangelism.

I've heard of a few churches that actually take their service times on a card with some candy and visit homes in the neighborhood surrounding the church. If you can organize this in your parish, that is a wonderful thing to do.

As a politician who has spent over a dozen years on my local town council and ran for higher office, I certainly understand door to door and how it works. But I would venture a guess that most folks reading this book don't want to go knocking on doors and I get it. Episcopalians tend to be private about their faith, and just as we wouldn't want somebody knocking on our door, we feel we would be imposing on them.

If your church currently does not do anything outside of its walls, this should be high on your priority list for the coming year.

Find a need in your community that is not being met and take that on. Even if you have a limited number of people in your congregation, two or three could get together literally and do a project, whether it's helping at the local book sale at your library, taking a shift at a local food pantry, or helping somebody clean their backyard out. Just do it and more will come! Remember; keep it simple and noncontroversial. I'm saying rather than go out and march in a protest, feed the hungry in your town.

You know it's very hard to invite somebody to come with you to a church service. I do it as often as I can, and over the years, a few of the folks that I brought in as a guest have become full-time members of the church. But it's a heck of a lot easier to invite friends and family to an event that your church is putting on.

I go back to volunteering at a local soup kitchen. If five or six people from your congregation brought a friend with them, it would show that your organization is doing positive work in the community and might inspire them to do more with you which eventually might lead to attendance at church.

When you have a special breakfast or dinner in your parish, that's a great time to invite people to come visit. If you do a Shrove Tuesday pancake supper, that's usually a no-brainer to invite your friends and their kids to come and eat. After they eat, give them a quick tour of the inside of your church. It can't hurt! And while you've got them there, you can let them know about what's happening the very next day on Ash Wednesday and maybe some of those people will come back and check you out.

So think about all of the special events you have during the course of the year. If you have a blessing of the animals, or a blessing of a first responder, or a vacation Bible school, or a Christmas pageant, use them as tools. Those are all great things to promote outside of your church that will bring non-parishioners in. Who doesn't want to go to the Christmas bazaar? Get them in the door.

Once you have them in the door, try to get their e-mail and address so that you can send a note thanking them for coming to your special event and letting them know that there are other things that go on in this great place. But you've got to get their contact information and you've got to follow up or they will not come back again.

It doesn't hurt to have items from your parish that identify you. Many of us don't mind putting an *Episcopal Church Welcomes You* sticker on our car window, so each parish should definitely have those to give to all of their parishioners. It's a statement, and the seal reminds people that when they see it, it is associated with our church.

Episcopal church calendars are great gifts at the turn of the New Year. Everybody wants a free calendar. So order them up and get your local funeral home to pay for the printing in exchange for an ad on the calendar. Make sure that your church name, address, website, and service times are clearly put in the blank space at the top of the calendar and you have something that people will see on a daily basis.

I know it's hard and I'm going to relate a story from my own experience. When I first started the communications committee at my church, I asked why we had so few calendars each year and why none of the calendars even had our name on it, let alone service times and contact information. The response was that it cost extra money to do that and we don't want to give them away to just anybody, only our parishioners that really want them.

Well, I don't mean any offense by it, but that was completely the wrong attitude. I don't want to print just a hundred of those things for our most faithful members. I want to print 5,000 of them and get them into every house in the community because I've never seen somebody refuse a free calendar. So the next year, we had service times, contact information, and location printed on them, and we gave away hundreds throughout the area. We learn by doing.

Does your community have a parade? Do you ever see that the local evangelical church always has float but you don't? That has to change. Get involved and make a float and buy some T-shirts that have the name of the church and make your presence known.

Do you have a town or city holiday event where people set up tables and sell their wares? Is there a festival in your community or carnival that comes to town once a year? Those are the kinds of things you should be present at and simply have something to hand each person. It can be a little card with service times, invitation to your next fun event, a pen, a magnet, calendar, or tote bag. Why not put that in their hands as they walk by and just smile and say that they are always welcome?

Another way of evangelism is to do something that any business would do. Join your local Chamber of Commerce and get involved. Every Chamber of Commerce has monthly meetings, whether it's an evening reception or a breakfast event. Get to know the leaders and business owners in your community and be a part of that chamber. They also usually have a local Facebook page and mailing list, and as a member, you can have your events promoted. So have your finance committee cough up the one hundred or two hundred dollars it costs to be a member per year and utilize all the benefits of chamber membership.

Does your local high school put on a fall or spring production? Do you have a marching band in your town? Do you have a venue that brings the arts to town? Be a sponsor of those places and take an advertisement in their programs. Usually, these things can be done very cheaply, and the rest of the town will see you support something that's important to them and it is a great form of evangelism.

Many communities, in fact almost all communities, have a public access television channel. Usually your local school board or city council/selectmen meeting is shown, as well as some possibly strange productions from other folks. But, remember, creating a TV show at public access is free, and they provide the training and they provide the equipment.

There's no reason that you can't get a group of people from your church and get a timeslot on your local cable access channel. At the very least, they have a community bulletin board that is digital and you should have all of your special events posted. All you need to do is send them the poster or the information digitally and they can pop it right in on screen. Doing a local TV or radio show is a great form of evangelism.

CHAPTER 5

The National Church—the Third Rail Which Is Gender, Race, and Sexual Orientation

If there is going to be a controversial chapter, then this is it. Yes, I am a white, middle-aged male cradle Episcopalian Republican. Read on knowing that it is my personal viewpoint, yet I believe it is a viewpoint many people with my background have but would never voice. My feeling is if you do not voice it, then people like me continue to leave. I also realize this is only my perspective. I also know we live in a culture where, if you have a conservative angle, the left will label you. That's fine. But our story needs to be heard, too.

I do believe in the structure of the Episcopal Church. It's amazing that the framers of our constitution in 1789—people like George Washington—are the same people that in 1790 formed our current denomination in the United States. We are pretty much the most uniquely American church there is.

We have a lot of great things in our history and have been very fortunate to be influential in our nation's growth and life. It's no small fact that our nation's cathedral in Washington DC is an Episcopal cathedral. Or that the largest cathedral in the northern hemisphere is St. John the Divine, New York City. Or that more than any other denomination, we have had the most presidents be Episcopalian. These are cool things, and I'm proud of all that. For such a small group, we have made some pretty big waves in our nation over the years.

I believe very firmly that the structure of our church is a good one with the house of laity and the house of bishops and the election of the presiding bishop to serve for a term of nine years. I think the timing of our conventions every three years is perfect, and I think the way in which we elect our delegates is also wonderful.

Where I think the national church has failed is that up until now each presiding bishop has pretty much ignored the decline and soldiered on in spite of it. Our last presiding bishop, Katherine Jefferts Schori, told us that "we're not dead yet," but again gave us no way to fix it. I have not heard a concise message from any presiding bishop directing us to restore our buildings, increase attendance, bring more people in, or for that matter, anything really practical that we can use. Ignoring the problem will not make it go away.

You know what? Maybe it's not up to the presiding bishop to do that all the time. Maybe it's up to the executive committee and those delegates that meet every three years and to the bishop of each diocese.

I think that the church's focus for the next ten years, which includes the next three conventions, needs to be to put aside differences and concentrate nearly 100 percent of our energy on reviving the church and growing the membership. And they need to put money and resources behind it.

We spend way too much time debating things like inclusive language, alternative liturgies, revising prayer books and hymnals, and apologizing to every organization or group that we might've offended in the past 250 years and so on down the road. We have a lot of infighting when it comes to elections, such as the use of the national cathedral the day after the inauguration in 2017 because people were offended by the president. Get over it.

We spend way too much time passing resolutions against pipelines in favor of caravans and defending this group or that group with some kind of proclamation. Stop it.

Remember what Paul wrote in First Corinthians. He pleaded that the followers of Christ set aside any differences for the common calling. Now is the time to do that. Now is not the time to fight over a new prayer book or anything like that.

Listen, our church fought against injustice. And we succeeded. We ordain women to the priesthood, we marry gay couples, we allow for no discrimination as to who can become a priest or bishop, and we even have been led by not only some great men but also have had a woman elected to the highest post in our church and currently now an African-American.

I think the strife is over, the battle done, and the victory of Christ is won. Sometimes it's hard when the war is over because so many people still have PTSD. But the war is over, and it might be time to move on to other issues. The Episcopal Church, if it stays together, can lead simply by example. We do the right thing, and it will catch on with the other denominations.

Our church is 90 percent white, a majority of the members make over a hundred grand a year, and we work in high levels of corporate America and government. And when these statistics are listed, it is as though that's a bad thing? It's bad to have money, power, and influence? I would think the Church would embrace that and use it to her advantage to do more good in the world. But, no, we are made to feel bad about our own identity. That's wrong. Too many middle-aged or old white people somehow equals bad. Keep that up and watch them all leave, along with their pledges. So many of them already have.

The other thing is since we revised the prayer book in 1979 all the way up through the changes we have made until recently, we have not grown the church. Instead, we have actually caused division and splintering, and it hasn't really gotten us anywhere.

We should now turn our attention away from revising the prayer book that does not need to be revised or worrying about if we call God a he or a she or Creator and concentrate on the basics. I don't need my pronoun written on my nametag at general convention. Knock it off.

I'm asking all of the delegates to put the social revolution agenda on hold for a few years and to not make any more liturgical changes for a few years so that instead of parsing words and pissing people off, we can proclaim the gospel to those who have left us and to those who we hope to convert.

There are many ways for the national church to get moving on this project. The first thing I would say is that our presiding bishop needs to visit more parishes around this country. There are only 6,500 churches which means, in the course of nine years, he or she should be able to visit a ton of churches and communities. Get out of New York City and move around the country. The revivals are a good step in the right direction.

What it means is for now probably the overseas trips should be limited, and we should really concentrate on the Episcopal Church in the United States and have him come to our parishes to inspire us.

It would be good if he could visit all of the fifty states so that people at least have an opportunity to get to one of his events. He's an inspiring leader, and I think if more of the people of our congregations across this country could meet and see him in person, we would be well served. We would be more apt to respond to the Jesus movement.

What I want our leaders to do is to stop talking about how we need to decentralized or downsize the church, sell the headquarters, etc., and really focus on inspiring each bishop and each parish priest to renew the call across our country.

We need to hear our leadership say there will be no more churches closed, there will be no more rectories sold, there will be no more ignoring decline. Instead, we will change the paradigm, and we will put our money where our mouth is so that we will grow.

We need the Episcopal Church to get the message out on a national level. That means a national advertising campaign. Out of the 320 million Americans, I bet you 2 percent are very familiar with our denomination, 70 percent know nothing about our church, and the other 28 percent probably don't know much more than what's written on the sign outside of an Episcopal Church building. It means we have a lot of work to do with branding ourselves.

I want to see an Episcopal Church ad play during Super Bowl. That's the kind of attention we need to get. We need to be out there. Every time you turn around, you should see a billboard that says the *Episcopal Church Welcomes You*. We need to make people ask, "What is this Episcopal Church all about?" I want to see us for the next three years promote ourselves like none other and like never before.

I want our national leadership to make sure that every parish has the resources to have a website and proper signage, and every parish has the ability, if they would like, to open a preschool or utilize their church buildings in other profitable ways that attract people and keep the buildings open. I want to see the Church offer a revolving fund for maintenance and repairs and other necessities. Instead of mission trips to the Far East, or Africa, or Europe, it's time to spend that money here shoring up our base.

If we could just stop debating race, gender, social policy, and politics for just one decade and take all of that energy collectively and pour it into evangelism, then we would be in great shape. Let us stop preaching *at* people and invite them in and listen for a while. Like Jesus did on the mountain, let us contemplate for a while.

The leaders of our church also need to understand that there is more than one segment of people that we need to appeal to. It's not just the refugee from Syria, or the gay parents who have adopted a child, or the inner city Hispanic teen who lost his parents. Those people are vitally important but not as the only focus of our church. I received an e-mail saying I should take a course to draw more Hispanics to the church. That's fine, but in my town, we are 95 percent non-Hispanic. Is this something I really need to learn? No. In Texas and Arizona and Manhattan, do we need it? Yes. Stop narrowcasting and start broadcasting!

We tend to forget about the silent majority. How about the middle-class white guy in Ohio who lost his manufacturing job and can't feed his kids? How about the single mom from New Jersey with the deadbeat husband? What about the run of the mill mainstream cradle Episcopalian that has a good life with no real issues but has been alienated from our denomination because he feels the church no longer speaks to him or wants him? Trust me, there's more than you know of those folks. It would do us some good to reach out to them, as well.

We are all children of God. Sometimes I think the church forgets that. Sometimes I feel like the church only thinks you are special if you are not from here or if you don't look like the stereotype of a typical Episcopalian. It seems like the only outreach is to find people that are different from what people think of as the traditional Episcopalian. What our leadership doesn't understand is that you need to do both. Not only do you need to reach out to new and diverse ethnicities, but you also need to reach out to your natural demographic, as well, to keep them in the pews. You do not need to sacrifice one for the other.

I have a problem with some of the advertisements and commercials that I have seen coming out of the national church. They all seem to perpetuate this picture of dreamy diversity that almost excludes much of the rest of what the church is. It's like you should feel bad if you live in a town that is fairly homogenous. Well, you shouldn't. You live where you live, and if you live in a town that is not diverse, it doesn't mean you're evil. But that's the way a lot of people feel they are portrayed.

In other words, in a multicultural diverse city such as Manhattan, Chicago, or Los Angeles, you might use one type of commercial, but then in suburban Iowa you may use another type of commercial, and in Chinatown you might use another. It seems like the national church has focused all of its attention on attracting segmented groups and not enough on the average mainstream lifelong Episcopalian. It seems like every time I read a post on social media from the Episcopal Church, it has something to do with race, or politics, or some kind of social justice issue. Sometimes we just need to be fed the gospel and not be preached at.

It's just not one size fits all. There are certain social justice issues that really resonate in New York that folks in the suburbs of Nebraska just don't relate to. It's not a one-size-fits-all Episcopal Church, just like it's not a one-size-fits-all nation.

And a lot of times the stuff that comes out of the national church sounds like it's meant only for people that live in the big cities or on the West Coast and forgets about the rest of the Episcopalians throughout *flyover* America.

The other thing I hate to say but I will say it is that allowing something such as gay marriage which affects probably 10 or 20 per-

40

cent of the population does not make a whole church. More people left the church over that decision than stayed.

And you know what? If you are against gay couples getting married, then you should leave the church, and if you are against women having equal rights in the church, then you also should exit left or right, whichever the case. But here's the deal. When our church just focuses on attracting homosexual couples to the church, or Asian Americans to the church, or Native Americans to the church, or whatever other group that they spend a lot of time and money trying to attract, they once again forget about all the rest of the Episcopalians in our country.

Now, believe me, if allowing same-sex marriage in our church brought 10 million more people onto her membership rolls, that would be awesome. But it didn't. And if having an African-American presiding bishop brought 1 million African-American members into our church, that would be great, but it didn't happen.

So the national church needs to stop talking about the color of skin and people's sexual orientation and rather just focus on the content of their character, as Martin Luther King said.

It's time to put on the color blinders and just try to attract any and all people to the Episcopal Church, in general, everywhere throughout our country—black, white, gay, straight, whatever. Let's build the church as a house of prayer for all people and stop acting like CNN commentators that do nothing but perpetuate race, gender, and sexual division. Not everything has to be an all-out knock 'em dead fight about some perceived injustice. The world is full of injustice. Get over it.

Recently, a church hung the letters LGBT from the rafters of the nave. My thought was, *Why?* We already include LGBT fully, why do they want letters hanging from the ceiling? I saw a post under the photo online from a man named Todd Lane, an Episcopalian from Connecticut, who wrote, "This is what annoys me about the Episcopal Church. As a gay man, I find it pandering and inappropriate. Would we hang *Straight* from our cathedral ceilings? Just #Stop!" I told Todd I could not agree more. And I can guarantee the majority of Episcopalians agree with Todd, also. And when I state that, I can

41

feel some of the very well-intentioned priests I have met are recoiling. Again, get over it and realize most of the people think *you* are wrong.

We also need to express to our leaders at the national church that changing our music or adding some alternative forms of worship don't attract new members. We have been trying this alternative stuff since the sixties and it doesn't work. Again, as I tell each parish, I tell the national church. Do what you do well.

Having churches change from playing the organ to playing the didgeridoo is not going to attract one extra Australian into our church (okay, well, maybe one or two). So let's just stop that stuff and reinforce our great musical history. If you are a High Church, then stay High Church. If you are Low Church, then stay Low Church.

Do what you do best, and the people will come. Try to change what you do best and follow some new national trend and we will fail as we have been failing. The church should not try to keep up with trends. Remember Pokémon go in 2016? Yeah, how long did that last? The church is something that should be solid as a rock, and it should exude our history.

Just remember every time you change something at the national level for a trivial reason or perhaps so that it doesn't offend two or three people that are bothered, you lose thousands of members. Eventually, when there's no one left and the church is 100 percent politically correct, then what are we going to do?

Here's what I want the church leaders to understand. You had 600,000 kids in Sunday school back in the sixties and now you're lucky if you have 100,000. And don't tell me it's because of declining population. There are a couple of hundred million more Americans here than there were back in those days. So we do have the potential to get more into our church.

Can our national church leaders focus on attracting parents and their kids to Sunday school? Can you give us the tools to reach out to parents of young kids and give us a reason that their children should be brought up in the life of Christ? Can you make a video about that so each parish can use it and not worry about exactly what color the people are in the commercial or what type of music you use in the background that may or may not offend somebody? Not everything we do needs to look like the bridge of the Enterprise on Star Trek. And I am a Trekkie.

Can you pass a resolution that insists that every parish try a vacation Bible school program within the next year? That's a resolution I can get behind. Why? Because VBS and programs like it actually work! It works even better if you invite those people to come to your church, as well. It gives them a great introduction. How do I know? Just recently, a family of four started coming to our parish full-time because the kids went to VBS last summer. It works. Pandering to subgroups doesn't.

I know my diocese had a resolution saying that during the course of the year 2017 we were to educate our parishioners on racial reconciliation and have three parish programs doing so.

So now we're on this kick to apologize for our role in slavery back in the 1700s. I was not alive back in the 1700s, and neither was anybody reading this book. I just think this backward-looking apology tour that the church is on has gone on long enough, and it's time to simply return to the basics. Look forward. Let's teach love.

I, for one, am sick of apologizing for being who I am. No one else has to, so why should I? I am not responsible for the ills of the past. I am not responsible for slavery or segregation in schools, or women not having the right to vote until 1919, or any of the social issues of the past which thankfully have been rectified. We closed our cathedral in the diocese of Rhode Island several years ago. The bishop had hoped a *center for reconciliation* located on the lower level would revive the cathedral. While there has been some mild success and I personally have contributed, there are still boards on the windows. It just does not work.

Let's get kids back into the church. Let's revive our Sunday schools. Let's revive our choirs. Let's revive our acolyte ministries. (Heck, when I was a kid we had so many acolytes at my church that I think I only got to serve once a month. Now I look up there every weekend, we're lucky if we have a crucifer; forget torchbearers.) Because we know when children are involved in something, it gives them a reason to come each week and to stay. It teaches them to see something through from start to finish.

They certainly don't want to be lectured about some problems the church had in 1750. We corrected those problems long ago and we don't need to rehash them. There is nothing to be gained. We are only going to alienate part of our base. They can learn that history in school. We need to be teaching about Jesus and his life.

Another resolution I would love to see is the national church challenging every bishop to double the size of his or her diocese in the next five years which means that every bishop will get on every priest and every priest will get on each vestry and every vestry will get on each member and that would have the potential to bear fruit.

I wouldn't mind seeing an incentive. Let's set aside one million dollars to the diocese that grows the most in the next triennium. At the end of those three years that diocese will get that check for one million dollars to be able to do good works in that locality. There has to be an incentive because, just like any other job, people get complacent.

You notice I haven't written much of anything regarding spirituality in this book. That's because I leave that to the people who are much more educated than I am in those matters. I would not presume to sit here and debate or lecture theology.

I'm looking at this from a survival point of view. I'm looking at this from a business point of view. I'm looking at this from a practical point of view. I love this denomination and what it has done and can do in the future, and I don't want to see it gone. I'm simply offering advice to those people who run the church at the highest levels.

I'm asking the national church to put aside small disagreements and focus only on growth. And when I say focus on growth, again, I mean let's bring home the one and a half million people that already say they are Episcopalians and let's get them back in the pews.

If we fail to do that, if we continue to alienate many of our members with pointless resolutions and further social justice issues that simply divide, then we are doing nothing more than reshuffling chairs on the deck of the Titanic because this ship is going down under if we don't change priorities immediately.

The Cathedral of St. John the Divine is the Cathedral of the Episcopal Diocese of New York and the fifth largest Christian Church in the world. Photo Credit: Bumbleedee

Christ Church, Westerly RI, is on the move, bucking the decline, and growing! Photo Credit: Ron Cowie

Christ Episcopal Church in Westerly RI is located in the historic downtown next to the Town Hall and Fire Station. Photo Credit: Chris Walsh

Trinity Cathedral in Miami Florida. Photo Credit: Galinasavina

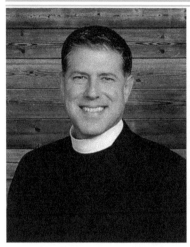

Fr. Alberto Cutie' also known as Padre Alberto is Rector of St. Benedict's in Plantation Florida. Fr. Cutie' is an author, radio and television host and commentator, most notably on the Telemundo Network.

Bishop Michael B. Curry is the 27th Presiding Bishop of the Episcopal Church, elected in 2015. He is a dynamic preacher and a breath of fresh air for the denomination. Photo Credit: The Episcopal Church

St. Bart's on Park Ave. in New York City is on the cutting edge of hospitality. They truly give meaning to the words "radical welcome" Photo Credit: Caswell Cooke, Jr.

An example of how a church sign should look. Fresh and new all the time. This is from St. George's in Griffin, GA Photo Credit: St. George's

The Cathedral of St. John in the Diocese of Rhode Island has been closed for several years. Boards are on some windows, but plans are in the works to re-open this place of worship by Bishop Nicolas Knisely and his staff. Currently The Center for Reconciliation houses the lower level of the Cathedral. Photo Credit: Caswell Cooke, Jr.

The author with staff at St. Martin's in Houston
Photo Credit: Christine Cooke

The author with Fox News host Tucker Carlson, a lifelong Episcopalian

The author with Kathy Johnson, Lay Minister of Membership
Ministries and Rev. Mary E. Wilson at St. Martin's
in Houston. Photo Credit: Christine Cooke

Contemporary worship service done right at St. Martin's in Houston TX. Photo Credit: Caswell Cooke, Jr.

St. Martin's in Houston, TX is the largest parish of the Episcopal church with nearly 10,000 members. Photo Credit: St. Martin's

St. Paul's Church in Key West, FL is a "magnet drawing
all people to the spiritual, cultural and recreational heart
of the community" Photo Credit: Tony Bosse

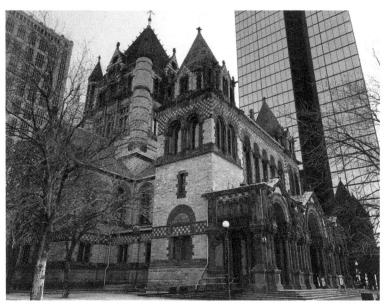

Trinity Church in the City of Boston, MA has a
congregation currently standing at approximately 4,000
households. Photo Credit: Caswell Cooke, Jr.

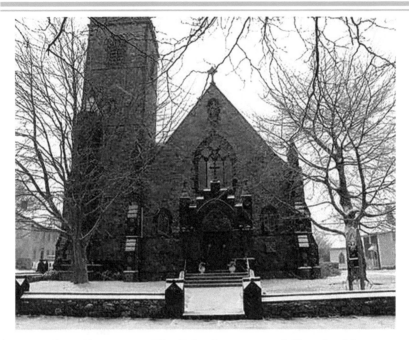

A white Christmas at The Zabriskie memorial Church of Saint John the Evangelist, Newport RI. Photo Credit: St. John

Fr. Nathan Humphries has more than tripled membership in just a few short years at The Zebriskie Memorial Church of St. John the Evangelist in Newport, RI. Photo Credit: Peter Silvia Photo

CHAPTER 6

So What Can Your Diocese Do?

Once the national church challenges each diocese to grow its membership, then it will be up to the bishop and his or her executive staff to make recommendations and preparations for the annual diocesan convention.

I would suggest that minor resolutions and argumentative changes be left off your diocesan agenda for these next three years and, besides your budget, clear it so that all of the time could be dedicated and focused on membership trends and how to fix the decline.

If your Diocese has a program that really works, such as my Diocese of Rhode Island where we have the Episcopal Conference Center camp and which in recent years has flourished, then put more energy into it so that it grows even more.

Make absolutely sure that part of your discussion revolves around advertising and what events throughout the diocese that the Episcopal Church can be involved in. You should also make sure that your diocese has the proper websites and social media pages, as well as a communications director.

Just as each diocese should be challenged to grow their church and receive a prize at the end, so should each parish within a diocese get the same incentive. The best thing would be a $50,000 award to the parish that grows the most. You might have two awards—one for growth in terms of actual numbers and one in terms of growth for percentage.

I said earlier that I encouraged the presiding bishop to stay put in this country for a couple of years and focus solely on the parishes in the United States (and diocese outside the U.S. that are under his leadership). I would also suggest that each bishop avoid a pilgrimage or sabbatical in the next year or two and try really hard to visit their churches even more frequently to really stay on each rector and their team and get to know even more about their parishes throughout their diocese. Obviously, if it's a small diocese with very few parishes, your bishop is going to have an easier job.

If your diocese has been focusing on a pilot program or some kind of mission work and spending a lot of money with no results, I would say end that and move toward helping established parishes get back on track and grow.

If it involves reducing a church to mission status so that the diocese can help with funding, then so be it. That could be a way for them to get back on their feet. It's worked before and it can work again.

I'm not here to tell the bishop of his or her diocese what to do. That's not something I even feel comfortable doing beyond a few suggestions. But I'm speaking here to the delegates, to your diocesan convention, and the clergy of your diocese. It is you that must insist that the diocese and the bishop spend a few years focusing solely on growth. When there are other items to talk about that can certainly wait, you dilute your agenda. Growth needs to be the only topic of conversation for the next couple of years or it will be too late.

I want each and every delegate and each and every clergy person to really take a hard look at the membership trends in the numbers since the 1960s in your diocese. You need to understand the severity of the problem before you can fix it. I guarantee it will be no fun to look at. I know at last year's Rhode Island convention where I am a delegate the membership slide was literally on the screen for thirty seconds or less, and it wasn't even talked about.

It's time for each diocese to really talk about it. It's time for each diocese to reallocate spending and put advertising at the forefront. It's time to rebrand each diocese if it hasn't had a rebranding in the last decade. It's time for the bishop to get out there and *press the flesh* like a politician to get people aware of our church.

I encourage each bishop to hold off on closing any more churches for the next three to five years, to hold on, and give your new direction a chance to work.

If your diocese is lucky enough to have an endowment, it might be time to consider pulling a few bucks out for some short-term promotion and the hiring of a professional advertising company. That advertising company in turn can help individual parishes that don't have the capability to pull off a website or advertising on their own at this point.

Your diocese needs to figure out what is best, but there should be billboards along highways, a presence at your state or county fair—if you are in a rural state—or if you're in New York City you need to get a billboard in Times Square. Your diocese needs to promote the Episcopal Church as much as possible, and you need to constantly be inviting people to visit one of your churches.

Your website needs to be completely up-to-date. Have a complete listing of every single church in your diocese that is accurate. Too many times our diocesan websites are out of whack. And if you don't have a diocesan website, then we need to talk privately after you read this book.

As the national apportionment is decreased, so, too, should the diocesan apportionment decrease from each parish to be fair. But rather than allowing that parish to roll the money back into their general operating budget, it should be earmarked for promoting that must be approved by the diocesan communications officer.

Once again, the national level it is too far removed from every day parish life to be of tremendous help to each individual parish. But on the diocesan level, that is the absolute best opportunity to do so. Each bishop should make sure that there is more than one person on their staff who is savvy with communications and send them out to each parish and basically enforce a standard that each church should have when it comes to social media platforms, websites, signage, and advertising.

Your bishop should not rest until every church is up to the diocesan standard. At the next general convention, each diocese can present their standards, and the best and most effective one can be chosen as the national standard of the Episcopal Church.

Your diocese should offer programs for the next two years for every vestry member, every committee member on how to be an evangelist. There should be training courses for social media and training courses for websites, and training courses for photographs and iMovies, and training classes for anything to do with promotion and growth. Forget the programs on sexuality and reconciliation for a while. They are nice, but they don't grow a church. Marching in a protest on city hall is not what I am talking about, either. That's easy. Do the hard work; don't be distracted by the trends of the day.

The diocese should insist that each church establish three committees. One would be a communications committee whose duties we spoke of in chapter 1. The second would be a lost sheep committee, and the third would be a welcoming committee.

CHAPTER 7

Shepherd to Lost Sheep

Every church has one thing in common. And that is lost sheep. Lost sheep are people that used to come to church but no longer do. The first thing you need to do to address this problem is start a *lost sheep committee* which consists of some of the elder members of the congregation who have long memories. It should also consist of some of the newer members of the congregation who are probably able to answer questions in a different light than a lifelong parishioner. So having a mixed group is good.

The second thing to do is to ask your parish administrator to let you look at all of the *inactive* members and to get a copy of all the address labels, as well as any parish photo directories from the past twenty years. Go digging if you have to and find where the old lists are hidden. Also be sure that you comb through any old guest books that may be located in your church to see if there are any valuable leads there.

The third thing you want to do is make a pot of coffee and sit down in a comfortable chair. It's going to take you a little while, but you'll be able to comb through all of this information and figure out who has passed away, who has moved to another town, and what you would be left with is a workable list of people that are going to need to be contacted.

You also want to see if any of these folks have children or grand-children that once came to church with them years ago and may now be adults themselves with their own children. You may want to find out where the children of your deceased members are living, too. Most of these next generation people will also have had some connection to the church, even if it was just for the funeral of their parents. But that is a connection. If they moved away and you have their new address, send it to the nearest Episcopal Church so that they can reach out. In the age of digital communications, this is easy!

The last thing is to ask for a printout of the e-mail list that your parish administrator is currently using and also if there are any old e-mail lists. Try to see if there are any people on this list that are not on your inactive list or parish directories from the past.

After a few meetings of this committee, you now have a list to work from. You're going to need to do a couple of things upfront just to test the information you have and make sure you have accurate addresses or e-mails.

Now it's time to design a very short letter which will also be e-mailed. In that letter you want to make sure you use the parish letterhead that is accurate with name, address, phone number, e-mail, and website. You can word it anyway you want, but the basic thing you want to say is "We just wanted to write to you to tell you that we hadn't seen you in a long time and that we were hoping everything was good in your life and just wanted to let you know that we are here for you anytime you need us." You can definitely go on to put the service times and rector's contact e-mail and phone number.

You could also include a return envelope with a little card and ask them to simply update their information, and for many of the parishioners who have been gone a long time, you probably don't even have their e-mail, so ask for that as well.

Then in a few days you will get people who have moved or are no longer alive (that you didn't know were no longer alive) back in the mail, and you can try other means to reach out by googling their name for contacting a relative to see where they are.

You will also definitely get some responses, and if you get renewed contact information put those folks in a priority pile. You may also get responses that are negative, so put them in a second pile. And then the rest that you get no response, take their addresses and separate them on the list called *second attempt needed.*

Now, as far as the e-mails, you want to do pretty much exactly the same thing. Put them all in a *lost sheep* list in your Constant Contact or Mailchimp account and write the same letter and send it out to them. If the e-mails bounce back, you know they are no longer in existence, and if you get a couple of people unsubscribing, then you definitely know what their answer is. But the rest of the e-mails that work, just go ahead and add them to your regular weekly or monthly distribution list so that those people get back in the loop.

You will have a list of people who returned new contact information, so those people need a direct phone call from the rector or somebody that the rector designates. They're going to need a phone call and a personal invitation to come on back to church and get involved. Whether you wait until homecoming Sunday or a special dinner event, there's some way that you need to get those folks back in church because they took the first step.

If you have some returns that have something negative about your parish, then the rector or one of his designees should make a phone call and determine what it was that upset them or caused them to leave.

Of course, there's national issues, such as gay marriage or other controversial things, that have recently become accepted in the Episcopal Church that may have driven them out. You can't do anything about that if they are not ready to accept all of God's people. But if it's something simple, like they might have been offended by the choirmaster, or perhaps an usher was rude to them, or they didn't like the last rector, or maybe somebody was sitting in *their* pew, you can address that concern. I'm joking about people sitting in the pew; it's an Episcopal thing. I know you get it. Sometimes an apology or an invitation to come back is all we need.

As for the group that didn't reply, just wait another month or perhaps two and craft a different type of letter and try it again. You may get a few more responses which you will know what to do with. But if you still get no response, then I would suggest possibly a phone call or maybe even a visit to their house if you know where they live. I know that's going to take a lot of courage, but that would truly be how you contact every last lead you have.

Let's face it. The people on this list are the people that are part of the census of three and a half million people telling us that they are Episcopalians. It's what we call low-hanging fruit in the industry. These are the folks you need to go after first. These people that have a history there, they have a connection in some way. That's a huge advantage and a start.

So, too, is reaching out to the children of deceased parishioners. Even if they were not raised in the church or did not attend very long when they were young, they still will have a connection to the place and it is still very much worth an older parishioner contacting them perhaps to just relay a story about something their mom or dad did for her at the church years ago that affected so many people. Sometimes a personal connection is usually always there, and it really takes a good chair of the committee to find out who should do the outreach.

And that is why every church must have a lost sheep committee. If the committee stays active, then as people disappear, you will notice it more quickly and be able to intervene in a more timely fashion so that you don't lose these folks for a period of many years.

One thing that our parish has done the past few years was to have a *homecoming Sunday* in September. Being a seasonal church (because, as we know, Episcopalians don't go to church in the summertime), when they come back in September, it's a big deal and it symbolizes things returning to a normal schedule after a busy summer. Cue the laugh track.

What we did is invite a former longtime rector to homecoming Sunday to preach. We had a full house in our church for the first time in a long time on a regular Sunday and many people who would not come since that rector departed were back in our church and we were able to get their new contact information and reestablish a relationship. Several of these folks have come back since that day.

We also forgot that this particular rector had done so much in the community that we had folks from the local Rotary Club and the local radio station and even a neighboring pastor from another church in attendance.

Very recently, noticing the Acolyte Guild was shrinking, we decided to revive the ministry. We began with an acolyte alumnae event where we vested nine former Acolytes who are now in their thirties, forties, and fifties and put them on the altar. We honored our former longtime acolyte leader who died twenty-five years ago, as well as our current retiring leader. We had all current acolytes vested and gave them all crosses. We made it known we are looking for more recruits. We also had over 200 people at that service where average for that time is 130. It works. We reengaged people we had not seen in years and put them right back to work. All we had to do was ask.

I know a few years ago the Roman Catholic Church had a *come home* campaign. Obviously, the attempt was to get people who relapsed and no longer connected to that church back in the pews. Some of the results of their advertising campaign are phenomenal. They had an ad during the History Channel showing of the Bible story on TV and said during that commercial they had 15,000 visits to their website. There were many more examples of the numbers when they launched the campaign during Holy Week. They had 75,000 visits to their website over a short period of time and many thousands interacting on social media. They really knew what they were doing.

There's no reason that the Episcopal Church cannot copy that successful campaign and do the exact same thing. After all, imitation is the sincerest form of flattery. It's like Coke and Pepsi. They're both a similar product, and they both need to advertise.

So we can see how this could translate on a national level and even a diocesan level, but how can you translate on a parish level? You can just do your own version of *Homecoming* or *Come Home* Sunday and get a dynamic speaker and make the service a little more special and invite people to come.

One last thing to think about and remember is that we have talked about posters and banners on social media and website promotion and newspaper ads, radio ads, and online ads. One thing we didn't do is talk about good old-fashioned snail mail. Now that we don't get half as many letters as we used to, it actually works to send a nice colorful postcard invitation to everyone on your mailing list when you have a special event like this. It is a cheap and effective way to reach out to lost sheep. Postcard stamps are not that expensive and it's a great physical thing for people to hold in their hands and to know that you were thinking of them. So in addition to all the cyber stuff we've covered, the good old fashion postcard works.

CHAPTER 8

Let's Roll out the Welcome Wagon

How many churches have ushers who give out programs or bulletins and take the head count? They provide a friendly face and some even show you to a good seat. We also many times have a hospitality committee which provides a wonderful coffee hour experience for so many people.

But how many times have you seen a person that you don't know come to church and maybe even to coffee hour and hardly anybody—in fact, sometimes nobody—speaks to them? Probably more often than we want to admit. One of the main reasons that people don't speak to them is because they aren't sure if that person is a member and just comes usually to another service and so they would feel embarrassed saying, "Hi, welcome," and that person turns around and says, "I've been here for twenty years."

Well, unfortunately, it's too bad if they've been there for twenty years and it certainly won't send them away, although it might provide a good chuckle for both of you. More often than not, it's a new person. And if they don't get a handshake or included in the conversation or asked if they want a cup of coffee, I don't think they're going to come back many more times.

So what you need at your church is a welcome committee. The welcome committee is not providing food and is not an usher handing out a bulletin. A welcome committee is a group of parishioners that make sure they scan the congregation for new people, and they make sure to speak to them in the church and especially at church events.

If you have enough people on the welcome committee, it's great if they actually went over and sat next to the newcomer. They might be able to help a little bit by showing them where they should be in the hymnal or prayer book or they just sit there to say hi and welcome them to the church. Sometimes to an outsider the service can be intimidating.

After the service, instead of running out the door, they could encourage this newcomer to fill out a pew card with their information or to sign the guest book in the narthex and they can invite them in to coffee hour where there should also be a second guest book.

The welcome committee is very important because it's the first impression people get. They should all have name tags. In fact, the welcome committee should be the ones that spearhead the whole parish membership having name tags. Name tags work and it puts people at ease.

The welcome committee should make sure that any information in the pews or rack cards in the back of the church or in the parish hall should be up-to-date.

I'll share with you a little story from my church. About a year ago I looked in the racks in the back of the church and pulled out a rack card and realized that it was from 1995 when our then junior warden was a teen. And it was about three or four rectors ago. That's terrible and that can't stand. So the welcome committee needs to be the ones that see what a visitor sees and make sure information is accurate.

They also need materials to hand to people. Not a ton of stuff but simplified. So if you have a couple that brings in a child or two, you want to hand them information on the Sunday school, or your chapel program, or even your nursery care that you provide. You should offer to lead them there, as well.

Let them know you have a comfort station for their baby in the bathroom located in the parish hall or wherever it might be. And if you don't have a baby diaper changing place in your bathroom, you need to get one. Not just in the ladies room—men change diapers, too. I know I did! These are the kind of things that the welcome committee can keep the vestry apprised of so they can put money toward items like that.

The last thing that the welcome committee can do is to translate some of these words that we use. Not everybody knows where the rectory is or even what a rector is. Certainly, a lot of people don't know what the narthex or sacristy is or a slype. And I bet undercroft is not on the tip of everybody's tongue. How about the sexton? I would never advocate getting rid of these wonderful words, but I do advocate letting the welcome committee act as translators.

We recently established the welcome committee at my church, and the chair has been very diligent about making sure that anyone who signs the guest book or fills out a pew card that their information gets put in the appropriate place. Number one, the rector gets a copy and sends out a note thanking them for coming. Number two, the office gets their information to add them to the e-mail and mailing list.

The final thing that the welcome committee does is organize newcomers' events. It usually works best if someone opens their home to the newcomers, and you invite them over for lunch or for an afternoon tea. Perhaps that sounds very old fashioned, but it's still kind of cool. Recently, our welcome committee had a nice event at the home of two newcomers and an additional six newcomers attended, as well as our rector and assistant rector and some members of our vestry. This kind of event had not been done in a very long time and it was refreshing and it was wonderful and it worked.

Two years ago our parish began teaching Episcopal 101 for those that are searching or want to learn more about the denomination or may be from a different denomination but have been attending an Episcopal church for a while and actually are thinking about being received. It worked—we confirmed and received people! We are ready to also launch Episcopal 102 for those folks who want to go deeper into the Episcopal Church world.

Your church needs to offer this course once a year, at least, and needs to advertise it. You need to invite people to it, and it needs to be interesting and needs to be fun. It's the only way to continue to educate people on the history of our Church and the mission of our Church. And I tell you what, it makes people feel a lot more comfortable learning about our particular brand of Christianity.

CHAPTER 9

Use the Church Property More

So many Episcopal churches are blessed to be so beautiful, and as I discussed previously, many are located in a prime spot in their town, especially in the Northeast.

We need to use our church buildings more. I don't mean for church functions; we already do that and we have many different functions throughout the year. What I mean is we need to use our churches for other things in the community.

We need to open up and advertise that we have a great space for so many uses. Lately, you've been hearing how churches are having yoga classes, or concerts, or renting out their space for wedding receptions, etc. This is the wave of the future. We have to rely less upon pledge income and more on outside income.

I'm going to share with you a story that is probably a microcosm of a very bigger problem that our church and that mainline Protestants have.

Our church is located in a beautiful downtown area in New England right across from the park and next to our Westerly town hall. We are probably the most prominent spot in the entire town. We are certainly in the most visible spot as far as our local churches.

On the front lawn we used to have a picnic table. A couple of years ago the picnic table disappeared, and when I inquired as to why, the answer was because people from the town hall on their lunch break were using it and they were not parishioners.

At that point, I really felt as though I needed to strangle somebody, but it just made me realize that the problems our church has to overcome are deep-rooted. Forget about reconciling the church with the history of slavery, how about we get the people that work for our church to let a neighbor use a picnic table? I would think that's more pressing. Imagine the message taking away that picnic table sent to the employees of the town hall. They certainly would never set foot on the property again.

Another example right at my own church was that a couple of years ago a group of homeschooled parents asked if they could use some of our Sunday school classrooms during the week once a month to get all of the area homeschooled children together in a group.

Our office did a really good job explaining why it was a lot of liability and they just didn't see how it could happen and those people were turned away. Imagine a group of thirty kids and sixty parents simply turned away because it might be inconvenient to have them use some unused rooms during the week. To make it worse, they were willing to pay!

What are these two little anecdotes tell us? It tells us if we're having this problem at our church in our town that it's happening many more places across this great nation. We have to stop being a group of people that looks inward and doesn't want to invite or share what we have with others. Easiest way to get new kids into the Sunday school and to get new families to come to our church would've been to roll out the red carpet for those homeschooled kids and their parents who wanted to use our facility.

It saddens me that we have wasted so many opportunities in so many churches because the stories are not isolated, they are the mentality of what is going on. I will say that since those two stories came and went, we have made great strides in being more welcoming as a center of community.

In recent years, our bishop has told us that we need to look for ways to use our facilities for more than just Sunday morning worship. So our property committee at our particular parish got together and came up with different rates for people to have events in our parish hall or in our facilities. It's a great way to make a little bit of extra money and to get people in the door. And we provide a less expensive alternative for people hosting parties and events or even wedding receptions.

Getting people in the door to use our facility gets them comfortable with the layout of the actual church. When someone is comfortable with a place, it makes them more apt to return on their own and explore what we do on Sunday mornings. It's a point first contact to get them in the door for something else.

It's important that your vestry and property committee sit down and go over every possible use of your church property.

When I was in Miami visiting the cathedral I ran into a priest who ran a smaller parish a few miles away over near Miami Beach. He said his parish was doing okay, but what was the saving grace was that they were able to rent out their parking lot during the week and that they had a preschool. Alternative uses of your property will provide a stream of income and make you more relevant in the community. I know it's hard to accept renting out a parking lot. We might stop and think, what has this come to? Let me tell you, it's much better to rent out a parking lot during the week so that your parish doesn't go under and you can be there on the weekends worshiping.

CHAPTER 10

A Quick Trip around the Church

This is a chapter that talks about my own personal experiences around the Episcopal Church in different areas. These are short notes, personal observations only, and critiques.

Saint Martin's, Houston

As you probably can tell by what you have read so far, I am upset that our church, as a whole, is in decline. I've always gone to church, and for the most part, you see less people as the years go on and not more.

So imagine my sheer delight when I went from little Rhode Island all the way to Houston, Texas, to Saint Martin's Church.

This is a parish with the membership over 10,000. You heard me right. Over 10,000. This is a church that is continually growing. This is a church that got so large that they actually needed to build a new bigger church and they fill it. On a pouring down rain Sunday, they nearly filled their contemporary service which was held in the old church complete with a rock band, as well as their traditional service, inside what looks like a cathedral complete with former First Lady Barbara Bush (shortly before she passed away) in the second row.

I was so inspired by being there and so happy to see so many Episcopalians. It was amazing to be in a place that was alive and vibrant. To see the ministries that go on at this parish, from feeding the hungry to drug addiction counseling, and even a school for little kids, was just such great hope.

I know that there are certain parts of the country where statistics show people are more religious, and certainly Texas is in the Bible belt, so naturally they would be more worshipers. But I don't think that's the reason people go to this particular church.

I think people go to this particular church because there is a message and there is a mission and they believe in something and stand for something. But they don't preach at you like the national church does; they preach the good news of the gospel.

A lot of my theories about advertising and social media probably don't apply at Saint Martin's, although they do have a membership director and they keep very good tabs on everyone that comes and everybody that visits gets a follow-up and they know who their members are and they work on that. So technology is important, but in their case advertising is not because so many people attend.

When I talked to vice-rector, the Rev. Martin J. Bastian, he was very clear about not only his own mission as a priest but in the mission of the church and the support of the rector of that church.

I would say if I took something away from Fr. Marty it would be that one of the downfalls of the church is that our clergy do not stay in one place long enough anymore to build community. He said people need to stay for ten years. He said it took him five years just to let people know that he was going to be there.

When I asked him what we should do about the shortage of acolytes, or choir members, or lay readers, he said you have to ask all the time. You can't just have *bring a friend to church* Sunday service once in a while because every Sunday has to be that way. He said if you know the families and if you have been in their homes, you have a relationship, and then you can ask them to be a part of the church organization.

For Saint Martin's in Houston, it is all about relationships and knowing the families and being involved in their lives and being a part of their homes and their graduations and their birthdays and their troubles and their joys.

I was absolutely floored to visit a church that did not have a membership decline and that did not have any sort of financial troubles. When you are in a great place you are able to think differently and, honestly, it was so refreshing and made me realize that it would be so nice to not have to struggle just to keep the lights turned on in the church building open.

I asked Fr. Marty if he would tell me one thing that the national church based in New York City could do to be helpful to the congregations around the country. His response did not shock me because I could not agree more. He said, "The national church needs to shut up and listen."

The national church, I think, needs to stop sending down their *moral authority* and stop telling congregations what they need to do to reconcile and apologize for the past. This particular parish doesn't do any of that. They actually just preach the Gospel of Jesus Christ as they live it out in mission in their community, and for them that is enough.

Trinity Cathedral, Miami, Florida

Trinity is a glorious building located in a wonderful and active city. Their Sunday morning service is beautiful. Trinity has a great choir, great preaching, and a very welcoming atmosphere. But in a cathedral that seats over 1,000 people, I was sorry to see no more than eighty in church at the main service and that included the choir and clergy.

After the service, it took at least ten minutes for someone to greet me and strike up a conversation. If I was a regular visitor I would have been long gone. I wonder how many churches around the country have the same issue. This is one area that can be fixed and should be fixed quickly.

I had a great conversation with the dean who was a few weeks from retirement. He told of how they raised literally millions to repair and revive the cathedral with so much support from the parish and community. That is no small feat in this day and age, so, again, something there was being done right. But, even so, with those attendance numbers, I don't know how long it can last. Let us hope the new dean will be able to raise the cathedral up!

St. Paul's, Key West

What a great place! Welcoming, warm, good music, and great preaching were what I experienced at St. Paul's. The week we were there they had a display that Buddhist monks were working on. We were made to feel welcome, and they certainly knew how to cater to tourists which must be a big portion of their attendees throughout the year. It was nice to see what, at least on the surface, appeared to be a healthy church.

The National Cathedral, Washington DC

Another place that is stellar. It really shows the Episcopal Church in its entire splendor. i have attended services there in the past and most recently brought my family to the nearly sold out Handel Concert. All I could say was *wow!*

The National Cathedral has the opportunity to showcase our church with large-scale national events, whether it is Presidents Ronald Reagan and George H.W. Bush or Senator McCain's funeral or a host of other national events involving the highest authorities in the land.

My fear is that we squander that by fighting over a Robert E. Lee stained glass window or a presidential prayer service. The National Cathedral should be a place to come together and heal; a place for conservative and liberal to meet. Instead, the cathedral has joined the National Church's call to arms for progressive social justice. It is a slippery slope for this great treasure to be on.

St. John the Evangelist, Newport, RI

This is a bright spot in a denomination that is losing its identity and declining. I went to St. John's and thought the Anglo-Catholic approach and mass was wonderful. What a great place! But it goes far deeper than that.

This was a parish that almost closed, was reduced to a mission, and turned it around and became a church again that is now healthy and poised for great things!

When Fr. Nathan Humphreys came to the church in 2013, the average Sunday attendance hovered around twenty-five people. Fast forward to 2018 and the average Sunday attendance was up to eighty-seven. In his first year, pledging was at 61,000, and for 2019 is over 220,000. Some years St. John's has had *over pledging* in the amounts of $25–$50,000.

I asked him in a nutshell what is going on to have this kind of growth and increase, and he said there are solid reasons. "The grace of God, truly, and the power of prayer are first. Preaching the gospel as the gospel and doing the work of an evangelist, being in the community, and, of course, the core people that were already there." He also admitted that the major factor is "money. We would not have been able to do this without the generosity" **of a few individuals in particular.**

He also pointed to the developing of The Choir School of Newport County. He described it as *an engine for growth.* The choir school is an innovative partnership created by three parishes, including St. John's. "Without doing any market research, we took a major risk by starting a choir school for the kids. It gets them involved and it brings along adults and pledging members, especially their parents. The kids have been the draw. All the choristers go to Sunday school during the service and come back at the creed." This engages the whole family. Fr. Nathan is optimistic about the future of his parish but still says it's going to take five million dollars over the next five years to do the things he needs to do. Good luck, and I know he will do it!

St. Bart's, St. John the Divine, St. Thomas, New York City

I've always had a fondness for Saint Bartholomew's in New York City on Park Avenue. Maybe it's because the wedding scene from the Dudley Moore and Liza Minnelli movie *Arthur* was filmed there or maybe it's because of the wonderful music or the great architecture.

I distinctly remember going there when I was a teenager one Sunday and being impressed by the welcome that I received as a visitor. It was sincere and remained in my brain all of these years.

I've been back a few times over the years but specifically went to check out the place recently and to attend two different services. One was a traditional service which I enjoyed very much and one was a contemporary service which I attended with some skepticism but left feeling good about. The alternate version of the Lord's Prayer put me off a little bit, I'll be honest, but gathering around the altar in the circle for more personal experience with the Eucharist was pretty cool.

I also noticed the demographics were a bit different at each service the day I attended. The traditional service was a bit older and skewed, more White, whereas the contemporary service was younger and had many different ethnicities in attendance.

Kudos to Saint Bart's for being able to offer something for everyone without taking away something from someone. This is the lesson the National Church needs to follow. Give the traditionalists the service they want, and give contemporary folks the service that they want. One is not more important than the other. One should not supplant the other.

I do think that Saint Bart's does tend to skew a bit liberal in its preaching and politics, but I do see a concerted effort to make everybody feel welcome all sides of the political spectrum. Some of the choices of books they have for sale give me a little bit of pause, especially the ones calling for the end of the white man. I can get over it.

I will also say that I did call the church and left a message and a couple of e-mails saying that I was visiting New York and wanted to check out the church and was writing a book and was hoping to speak to one of the clergy. I never did receive any response, so hopefully that mistake will not be repeated in the future for persons looking for pastoral care, for instance.

All in all, I think that Saint Bart's is definitely a light in the darkness and has learned to use their building wisely and has learned to bring in alternate sources of income and really takes the mission of feeding the hungry to heart. I would recommend people visit this church when in New York City to learn about radical hospitality and welcome.

As a side note, whenever I am in the city I also try to take in Evensong at Saint Thomas Fifth Avenue. What a beautiful place and a beautiful choir and what unbelievable glorious tradition. Attendance doesn't seem to be very good for these events, so I hope they can really work on that because it would be terrible to lose such a great tradition.

Saint John the Divine Cathedral is another wonder of the Episcopal Church. It is the largest cathedral in the northern hemisphere. I've gone there many times over the last thirty years since I was a kid. I love that wonderful place.

They really are a cultural and arts mecca in that area of the city. Their programming is wonderful. Again, I think the politics are very left-leaning, sometimes they make headlines for controversial artwork, and some of the things they choose to crusade for are divisive, but that cathedral does wonders.

My hope for the cathedral is that they could take care of the building better and really try to focus on raising funds to get the place completed in this lifetime, at least. Looking at the building from the outside, it is usually filthy and looks to be in disrepair, with scaffolding and other things going on. It's a far cry from the look of our National Cathedral in Washington. If there's a way for the diocese to focus on getting the cathedral in good condition, it would be an effort worth the undertaking. Again, this is a microcosm of the whole church.

If we fix our own roof and take care of our structure, we can better serve others from a base of strength.

It's harder for me to tell a large church in the city what they should be doing. Even though I was born in a large city, I have lived in a small town my whole life, and so I'm probably better suited to talk about the majority of parishes in the Episcopal Church but not the ones in the downtown city setting. Obviously, if they have survived this long, they are doing something right. They're also adapting to the cultural and demographic shifts and learning to forge ahead.

My only advice is for them to try to be as center as possible, politically, and to try as much as possible to follow what Saint Bart's is doing.

While I was in this New York state of mind—no pun intended—a Billy Joel song came on the radio. And the words reminded me of the Episcopal Church of late. The Episcopal Church leadership being the Angry Young Man.

"There's a place in the world for the angry young man
With his working class ties and his radical plans
He refuses to bend, he refuses to crawl
He's always at home with his back to the wall
And he's proud of his scars and the battles he's lost
And he struggles and bleeds as he hangs on the cross
And he likes to be known as the angry young man
Give a moment or two to the angry young man
With his foot in his mouth and his heart in his hand
He's been stabbed in the back, he's been misunderstood
It's a comfort to know his intentions are good
And he sits in a room with a lock on the door
With his maps and his medals laid out on the floor
And he likes to be known as the angry young man
I believe I've passed the age of consciousness and righteous rage
I found that just surviving was a noble fight
I once believed in causes too
I had my pointless point of view
And life went on no matter who was wrong or right
And there's always a place for the angry young man
With his fist in the air and his head in the sand
And he's never been able to learn from mistakes
So he can't understand why his heart always breaks
But his honor is pure and his courage as well
And he's fair and he's true and he's boring as hell
And he'll go to the grave as an angry old man."

Can you read that all the way through and see how it relates to the direction of our National Church? Are we angry at the world because we want to be? Are we angry because that is easier? I think the answer is yes. Sometimes we have a pointless point of view because we are desperate to be relevant. It's harder to be realistic.

CHAPTER 11

A Conservative Voice in the Wilderness

I got to thinking that so many people that are Episcopalian and are prominent these days are on the left, politically. So it kind of surprised me to know that Fox News' Tucker Carlson is an avid Episcopal Church member, as are his wife and children. I learned that Tucker went to St. George's Episcopal School in Newport, Rhode Island, in the state that I live and I thought he would be someone great to talk to about how he feels in this political climate being a member of the Episcopal Church. This was almost kind of a reverse test case, if you will.

To my delight, after I e-mailed his office, he quickly agreed to talk to me, and we had an awesome phone conversation that went on for almost an hour and I could really feel his genuine love for our church and especially the parish he attends.

I will tell you, though, that he, too, agrees with me that the Episcopal Church is on a trajectory toward collapse, and he thinks that just about the entire leadership of our church is to blame. "The church is dying. That's not even a point of speculation. Look at the numbers."

He had very harsh words for the leaders in the Episcopal Church and when I asked him if he was sure that I should print exactly what he said about them, he reiterated and doubled down and said yes. "One of the main problems with the Episcopal Church is that it is staffed heavily by losers."

Now let's break down that statement. We know that Tucker is involved in a business where contentious statements like that are the norm. Watching Fox News or MSNBC on a nightly basis will show you that both sides are out for each other. So if you can get beyond the insult of what he said and get to the root of why he said it, you might find some sense. If you can't then you will recoil in disgust, put this book down and use the usual talking points of racists, misogynists and so on. But if you can breathe, read on. And read on knowing that probably upward of half the people you worship with on Sunday also watch Fox News. Maybe not All Saints in Pasadena, but in most of the rest of the country.

I spoke off the record with a bishop in our church who said that one of the main problems he has is that over 50 percent of the priests in his diocese are not up to par. They are either burnt out or are not committed to mission, and therefore they contribute heavily to their church failing. So there is a back up to the statement that the church is staffed heavily by losers. I'm not sure that I would use the word losers but the sentiment is the same.

One of the other issues is that back in the old days people became a priest and that was their life vocation. Nowadays, the trend is more toward middle-aged folks like me going to seminary and becoming priests. There's nothing wrong with middle-aged people becoming priests. But if it's one of the rungs on your personal growth journey and if being a priest is one of the steps in your twelve-step program, then you've got an issue and the church has an issue.

And we can see that coming through now. Tucker says that so many priests don't have *their personal life squared away*, and that backs up what the anonymous bishop told me.

Carlson further breaks it down saying that "Liberal Protestantism is over. It's been going on for decades. It's a joke." When I pressed him on this point, he further explained in his own words, "The point of Christianity, if you were to boil it down, it answers the question of death. What happens when you die? It's not about feeding the homeless, although I think that's great. It's not about feeling virtuous, it's about answering that question."

So how does that affect church attendance is what I wanted to know. Carlson said, "No one is going to get up on a Sunday and put on a tie and go to a place where they don't answer that question. I mean, why would you? You wouldn't. One reason the church is dying is that the people that run it don't believe that core message and the people in the pews know it, so they go somewhere else."

All right, so it's easy to lay blame at the feet of others, and it's easy to find out, broadly speaking, what is wrong. So I asked him more poignant question. Why do you, Tucker Carlson, stay in the Episcopal Church?

"The first reason is inertia. My father-in-law is a priest, and I've been there my whole life. My kids were baptized there and my wife attends daily.

"The second reason is the liturgy. I sincerely love the liturgy. It is totally meaningful. It's the sum total of a lot of thoughtful reflection. I don't think the words are accidental. Words are meaningful to me, in general, and I think that our liturgy is one of the great gifts to Christianity and the world. Ours is the best."

The final reason is something we can all derive a lesson from. Tucker has been going to Christ Church in Georgetown since high school. He said about his family, "We like our church and that's the most compelling reason to stay."

Carlson further goes on to explain, "Our parish moved away from the dividing lines in the National Church. Our parish has chosen a different approach and that is to retreat back into the core of the faith, if you will, of the denomination which is the liturgy and our collective celebration of it. That's what I'm comfortable with, even though I have a job that is exceptionally confrontational and political. But that's not what I want to see on Sundays at all. Our parish is healthy, we have no debt, it's pretty full, and families are engaged. That's what you get when you focus on the core mission."

So maybe if we take a deep breath and step back and realize that just like our country, probably half of our church feels the same way as Tucker does, then we could all take a lesson from that. Maybe engaging all of these social justice movements in the name of ourselves rather than in the name of our church is the better way. Don't speak for others sitting next to you in the pew and don't judge them either—lest you be judged. We all arrive in the Episcopal Church for our own reasons. Respect that.

CHAPTER 12

Another Way of Doing Things

Father Alberto Cutié was born in Puerto Rico and has been an Episcopal priest for the last decade. Before that, he was a Roman Catholic priest for fifteen years. He is internationally known for his media appearances and as an author, among many other things.

Fr. Cutié began his ministry in the Episcopal Church at the Church of Resurrection in Biscayne Park, in Miami, Florida, where he stayed for six years. When he arrived there were twenty-eight parishioners, and when he left there were over 250, and the congregation is still going strong five years later.

I asked him what he did to revive this parish, and he said he went into the community to see what the needs were and told everyone that there was a vibrant church there. His mission was to provide welcome worship, good music, and, as he jokingly said, *semi-good preaching*. He said he revived the traditional Anglican organizations within the church, such as the ECW and the Men's Group, the youth group, the Sunday school, and all the basics. "We started resurrecting them one by one."

One of the things that he thinks the Episcopal Church needs to do is to *acknowledge the Latin explosion and to be on top of it*. What he did at that church was to have a service in English, as well as a service in Spanish. He didn't take anything away from the English-speaking folks, he just added another service. When he left there were about one hundred people going to the English service every weekend, and 150 going to the Spanish-speaking service. The demographics of the area that he served warranted a multilingual church.

When I asked him about the trend of shutting down conservative voices in the church, he enlightened me by saying, "We need those voices because one of the things we are doing is alienating ourselves. We say we are a big umbrella, but if anyone comes from the right and seems conservative, we blow them off. If we're going to be the big umbrella, then we need to be the big umbrella for everything, not just what is convenient to us." Father Cutié's current parish, St. Benedict's in Plantation, Florida, was, as he described, *the first parish I got to that was not in crisis mode.*

He said there were some issues in 2003 when the vestry voted to build a new structure which is their current church, and also some left over the sexuality issue in the National Church when Bishop Gene Robinson was consecrated as the first openly gay bishop. His transition was very smooth, and he described it as a *healthy parish and an Anglo-Catholic parish which is now a bit more of a broad church, but still on the high side.*

When he arrived, average Sunday attendance was 350, and now they have seen steady growth and are averaging 500 people per weekend, with three services in English. "We are what the Episcopal Church dreams about when they speak of diversity. We are Black, White, Latino, and Anglo. Every weekend there are people from over fifty-five countries worshiping in the pews. People are from all over the Anglican Church, especially the islands. But at the end of the day we are one family. We are a microcosm of America."

I brought up, of course, the question of the National Church and the trend toward dealing with and taking on all social justice issues.

His take was the following: "We engage in social justice issues as they relate to the gospel. What I do differently is we are not going to preach pro-or anti-Trump sermons. I couldn't care less who the president in the White House is at the moment because I have too much to say about Jesus to worry about that. We spend a lot of time focusing on the gospel and certainly for the most part I do not engage in alienating people on the left or the right."

As far as dealing with the latest hot button issues, Fr. Cutié said, "We are just not that kind of parish. I find too many of my colleagues throughout the church are very much in tune with what's happening in politics and spend a lot of pulpit time dealing with whatever happened this week in Washington, and I'm not so sure that's the mission of the church."

Fr. Alberto went on to say, "We invite people to think for themselves, not tell them how they should be thinking according to our own agenda, left *or* right."

We got on the subject of the National Church, and he pointed out that Presiding Bishop Curry has done the church a great service because he focuses on Jesus and "The more he emphasizes the *Jesus movement* and the gospel the better it is for everyone in the church."

He doubled down and said again that the national leadership and local vestries "need to have people from every tendency, otherwise we continue alienating people. The church has to be serious about diversity. Are we really open to everyone? We have to stop having liberal and conservative diocese and bishops because it doesn't serve the gospel."

We touched on ethnicity and how his parish is very diverse, but many parishes across the country are not. His response was, "Your church does not have to have ethnic diversity to be sensitive to it."

And the subject of prayer book revision, Fr. Cutié said, "I have 500 people every Sunday at my church. I'll tell you, 99 percent of the people are happy with the prayer book the way it is. I just see it as an excuse for the church to waste more money."

A full prayer book revision doesn't necessarily mean that our language can't be more inclusive, as he went on to say, "I see the need for inclusive language and I try to use it where I can, but I think it's an agenda of the theological elite in the church" who parse every word.

We were talking about the most recent General Convention of the Episcopal Church and how, after the discussion on inclusive and non-masculine language, there was an interview that Bishop Curry was doing and the reporter asked him, "How will you pray the *Our Father?*" Cutié said, "He replied, 'I will pray the *Our Father* the way I have always prayed it. Our Father who art in heaven.'" Enough said.

He further went on to say, "Telling people how to pray that is gender neutral is almost arrogant. To impose gender one way or the other is what I don't like."

Our conversation moved to the National Church and the topic of growth which, of course, is what this book is about. "It's wrong for the National Church to come and say this is how to do things. I don't think that works. The church is universal, but the church is also local. You have to pay attention to the local need."

Fr. Alberto said that our diversity of low and high church and left and right is a great gift, but "how do you manage it day today? There is no magic formula."

He said the way to growth is not through hiring consultants. "It is shameful to spend so much money on consultants. Jesus gave us more than any consultant will ever give us. He gave us the mission and the vision of the Church. We need to go out and proclaim the good news, baptize, feed the hungry, heal the sick. It's shameful to spend money and resources on a consultant who will take your watch to tell you what time it is. It's a huge mistake."

One of the things I frequently get into arguments with people about is how much advertising the church should do. Should we really be on every billboard and in every newspaper? Should we be advertising ourselves like we are advertising a restaurant? I brought this up with Fr. Cutié to see what his perspective is since he has a thriving growing parish.

He started off by saying that "have you ever heard of scenario planning where they pay someone to tell you how in ten years your church is going to fail? There is such thing as a self-fulfilling prophecy! Instead, you can say, what can we do to turn this thing around? What can we do to make this better and what can we do to bring in new people? If you put your energy into that instead of planning for the worst-case scenario, you're going to grow. The church is not a sinking ship. It's filled with hope for the future."

What's the best way to do this, I asked? He said we have a wonderful gift because the presiding bishop is such a great speaker and such a great motivator, and we should be buying TV time on all the major markets on Sunday mornings and showcasing the Episcopal

Church and how it welcomes you. He commented on how evangelical preacher Joel Osteen has a half hour program on a Sunday morning and has 20,000 members of his congregation.

With the Episcopal Church and all of its resources, why can't they do the same thing? Why can't there be a half hour with the presiding bishop "just following him around doing what he does so well—preaching love, preaching the Jesus movement?" Fr Alberto said we should have this going in Miami, Los Angeles, Chicago, New York, Houston, and all the other major markets. "The world is filled with new ways of communicating, why shouldn't the church be at the front and center of that? We can't be a twenty-first century church acting like it's still the eighteenth century."

Finally, our conversation turned to leadership. Fr Cutié said, "A rector that can't bring people together should do something else" with their career. He said the same thing goes for bishops. "Leadership impacts the church. If you keep doing what you're doing, you're going to keep getting what you're getting. If you choose the safest person to be a bishop or a rector, you won't see change. Are we really interviewing the people we choose for bishops? An interview is not a walkabout."

He points to Bishop Daniel G. P. Gutiérrez, the bishop of the Episcopal diocese of Pennsylvania since 2016. He said he is amazing with his cheerleading and his social media prowess. He sets a great example for what many other bishops should follow.

Fr. Cutie said that all of the churches have been losing members. It's not necessarily for one particular reason or another, it's just that people don't attend church the same as they did in the 1950s and 1960s. He said the Catholic Church experiences the same exodus of members. However, they have been far quicker to embrace Latinos and much better at it than most of the mainline Protestant denominations. "The ones that are growing where the white Anglo population has stopped coming are the ones that are embracing the Latino population and the immigrants. The Episcopal Church's embrace of immigrants has been much slower, and that impacts our numbers."

He went on to also talk about how you *build up the church in the mainstream* and he said it's *one parish at a time, it's one case at a time, one member at a time, one family at a time.* If you're there for them at a funeral, if you're there for them at a time of crisis, these are the things that will bring people back into the church.

Amen, Fr. Cutie!

CHAPTER 13

The Big Question: Will This Decision or Change Grow the Church or Cause It to Lose Members?

I firmly believe that if everyone in authority in the church, whether it's at General Convention, diocesan conventions, or the parish vestry level, or whether it's bishops, priests, and wardens, ask that one question before they make each decision. It will be a game changer.

Let me list a few examples. If we change the prayer book to reflect God as gender neutral, will any new members join our church? Doubtful. Will anyone leave our church? Yes. If you change the Lord's Prayer to "our Creator who art in heaven," thousands of people will walk. *Not* because they are against women but because they love tradition. There is absolutely nothing to be gained by changing the language.

No current Episcopalian is going to leave the church if we do *not* change the language. Think about that. Please refrain from screaming and jumping up and down and being offended. Just go up to 20,000 feet and think about it. Will the decision to change the language grow this church? The answer is a resounding no.

The questioning of leaving the American flag in the church or removing it to the parish hall or to some other non-religious part of the building has been brought up at some churches. If the flag is moved, will any new people come into the church? No. If the flag is moved, will some people get angry or offended and leave the church?

Yes. Will anyone who does not like the flag in the church leave if the flag stays? No.

Last year the Diocese of Rhode Island had only one resolution that was presented at the convention. The resolution dealt with the number of immigrants that should be let into the country. This is once again something that will do nothing to attract members to the church and will only cause members to leave. I am not going to ask for resolution to build a wall along the border, but also I don't want a resolution telling me to tear it down. That's a political mess that our diocese and our denomination cannot afford to get into. It's just not worth it. There are so many ways we can serve the Lord. We do not need to pass resolutions and send them to politicians who won't even read them, while at the same time alienating half of our own members. In a cultural civil war, which this nation is in, the Church cannot take sides or there will be a civil war within our church.

As a side note, if you are so passionate about an issue, join the Red Cross, or Amnesty International, or the Peace Corps. Please don't turn our church into a radical leftist political action committee. That's really my point lately. The church and its Episcopal Public Policy Network should really rethink their tactics and watch out when they are speaking for the entire membership of the denomination. Yes, General Convention may authorize it, but sorry to say General Convention as of late is woefully out of touch with rank-and-file Episcopalians.

Back to the immigration resolution. I have to say that thankfully in our church with the type of democracy we have I was able to attend a workshop that discussed the budget and resolution for the convention. I waited through the budget process, which I thought was very well explained, and then I listened as a person explained the immigration resolution. I was given a chance to speak and pretty much expressed what I just said; that I don't think this resolution is going to do any good for anyone and it may simply cause division within the diocese. I also expressed concern that the author of the resolution was not there to talk about their own resolution.

When I was finished speaking and mentioning some of the points that I have made here in the book about membership decline and where our focus as a denomination should be, I was approached afterward by almost everybody who thanked me for making the journey to the meeting, which was definitely on the other side of the state and out of the way, and for bringing up an alternative view. Actually, many of them shared this view but were afraid to express it. Again. the silent majority of the church isn't encouraged by the politicking at the diocesan and national level.

On the other hand, individual congregations who serve large immigrant populations are awesome. There was one rector of a church who came up to me after the meeting and said that their focus, because of their changing neighborhood, was to reach out to a new immigrant population coming into the community and help them with food and housing. That is definitely the work of God. There's no politics there; it is simply helping people that are already here and bringing them into the religious community.

There's another great story out of Tennessee that many of you may have heard about from the 2017 movie *All Saints*. This is the story of a dying church that had about a dozen members and the new rector decided that instead of closing the church he was going to reach out to the new immigrant community from Asia who were Anglicans and in need of a church and of a way to grow crops. He started a farm on the property of the church and turned that place around and brought together the entire community. But, again, there was no politics involved and there were no resolutions being passed from the National Church. It was an organic renewal of a church and that is the way it should be. It wasn't forced; it was natural.

This past year the diocesan convention was no different. One resolution was submitted—the immigration and asylum resolution again. The other event was to pause Convention at 11:15 to send off protesters with a litany to attend an LGBTQ rally on the state house steps in Providence. Again, let anyone who wants to go to the rally go, but you don't need to pause and send them off with a litany! I don't think they would stop and send me off with a litany to go to a pro-life rally. So stop kidding each other. There is an agenda, it represents half the church members, and it has to stop or it will drive the other half out. For the record, I did not attend the convention.

Instead, I used my position as delegate and sent a note to the bishop telling him my absence was a silent protest of the church going off the rails of the crazy train. I had much better ways to spend my Saturday than being in that scene.

Our particular parish takes part in a program called Operation Christmas Child. Basically, you fill a shoebox with presents, and they are sent to children in need in other countries. It's a great program and it's helped many people over the years. At my parish there are four ladies who have really taken this project on and made it very successful and are passionate about it. It is one of the ways that they show their love of God in ministry to the world.

At one of our vestry meetings a member said that we probably should discontinue this program and look for an alternative program because the ministry was connected to the Rev. Franklin Graham. And she added, "Certainly, we cannot be associated with views like his." Well, I almost leapt out of my chair at that point. I mean, really, are you serious? I said, "Let's all stop for a minute and think. If we get rid of or change this program, will any new people come to our church? No. If we get rid of or change this program, will it upset people or cause them to leave our church? Yes. Is this program hurting anyone or helping anyone? The answer is that it helps people."

Our church constantly preaches that we are supposed to accept people that are different from us and accept people with different viewpoints. But right there shows that if the viewpoint is different from that of the National Church, which is extremely left leaning, then that opinion is no good and against God's will. The National Church assumes they always have the moral high ground.

Well, let me thankfully say that the vestry unanimously voted not only to table the issue but to never bring it up again. We commend those parents for putting together such a vibrant program each year and supporting children in need around the world. But this is a microcosm of what is going on all over the church. We are losing members because we are making poor decisions that we think are right based on our political or personal beliefs. We preach tolerance as long as we all agree with each other. The minute somebody comes up with an opposing viewpoint that is conservative, we want to throw them out the window. This has to stop.

Time and time again the church wades into political quagmires that will never have a good outcome. Let's think about the fact that the current President of the United States, when he does choose to go to church, goes to an Episcopal Church. He was married to his wife in an Episcopal Church. Yet our National Church spends most of its energy railing against one of its own parishioners. So on Christmas Eve when the President of the United States walked into the Episcopal church near his estate in Florida and received a standing ovation, were all those parishioners bad Episcopalians and bad people that need to be purged from our membership rolls? Think about that. The National Church basically is saying if you support the current administration you do not belong in the church. I am not defending the current administration but I am saying railing against it is not the answer, either. And let's not start on another Episcopalian Supreme Court Justice Neil Gorsuch. I'm sure leadership wants him out, too!

It's not that anyone is bad or trying to do harm. They are trying to do good things. But the resources are being used in the wrong place. I recently saw that St. James Episcopal Church in Cambridge, Massachusetts, was hosting an anti-oppression lessons and carols for epiphany. They actually have a group at the church called an anti-oppression team.

Now, to be fair, I have never been there and don't know much about what they do. This is the kind of good intentioned thing that is just the wrong use of resources. It's time to do something that is actually going to get people in the door and stop trying to create a kumbaya moment that is fake. It's trying too hard to recreate the 1970 Coke commercial where all of the world stands on a mountain and sings *in perfect harmony.* Give me a break.

Just perusing the Episcopal Church national website, every single item has something to do with division and conflict and perpetuating it. Whether it's protests at Standing Rock, caravans heading toward the border, or changing the name of the church because it was the home of a Confederate general, or dedicating a stained glass window to LGBTQ ministry, or constantly pushing racial reconciliation, which in my opinion causes more divisions, every item is politically motivated and left-leaning. Again, I'm going to say that there is nothing wrong with LGBTQ ministry, and there is nothing wrong with racial reconciliation. But when that is the only thing being talked about, it's a problem. When it is shoved down our throat, it is bad. We need again to be broadcasting our message, not narrowcasting to groups.

It's time to stop. None of it works. We are losing members because of it. We are not gaining members because of it. You basically have a church leadership that is yelling at its 90-plus percent White membership that they are no good and they are the cause of all the problems of the past and that they need to apologize for being who they are.

Can't we just stop it and move forward and preach the gospel and evangelize and concentrate on teaching our children about the faith and get back to the basics? Why does everyone have to be inserted into a category? Are we not all children of God? If we say that the Episcopal Church welcomes you, why do we also need to say, "And gay people and black people and white people and straight people?" What don't we get about welcomes *you*?

I mentioned it previously, but it's worth mentioning again. There were truly some great struggles in the church, first of which was our participation in the Civil Rights Movement in the sixties, ordaining women to the priesthood in the 1970s, followed by same-sex marriage, and ordination of openly gay clergy in the 2000s. These were huge steps which, of course, caused division, and it did cause people to leave the church. But I, as most of us who are still here, believe that these decisions needed to be made and, in the end, will be beneficial to the church.

But now I must again implore the same people who won this battle to be gracious in victory and, having done what was right, just let it be the norm rather than continuing to draw attention to individual groups within the church. Can't we just say that Rev. so-and-so was elected Bishop of Connecticut or Bishop of Southern California? Why does it always have to be *the first Black woman,* or *all-female slate,* or *an openly lesbian person,* etc., etc.? Who the hell cares, if they do the job? When can we stop and just focus on the person and the job they are doing in the church instead of always calling attention to race, sexual orientation, and gender? It is time to move on to the next chapter. A friend of mine mused, "Are some people privileged? Yes. Are some people subconsciously prejudiced? Yes. Check the box, move on, what can we get done together?"

Maybe another way to look at some of the decisions the church makes is to offer more choices, not less. For instance, if and when the prayer book is updated, would it be so bad to have a chapter for traditional marriage between a man and a woman, and then a chapter for marriage between a woman and a woman, and then a chapter between a man and a man? Would that make too much sense? Rather than changing the current version for traditional marriage, simply add language separately for different types of services. Then nobody gets upset because you have not taken anything away, you simply added something. Instead of shoving it down a straight person's throat by forcing them to change their language to prove someone right or wrong, just add another rite!

Remember when we used to say, "Glory be to the Father and to the Son and to the Holy Spirit, as it was in the beginning is now and ever shall be world without end. Amen?" Then we watered it down and changed it to "is now and will be forever," and we offended a lot of people for absolutely no reason. Wouldn't it have been better to keep that original language from the 1928 prayer book in Rite I and have Rite II be contemporary? Of course not, that would have been too smart. And God forbid we keep the Holy Ghost! The Episcopal Church likes to throw the baby out with the bathwater.

All of these people that get angry and want to use the 1928 prayer book still...wouldn't it make sense to have the '28 version of the service and the '79 version of the service, and then a 2019 version of the service? Rather than say, "No, you can't have what you are currently doing" and "You can't have what they did in 1928," you can only have what we deem is good for you now—the wrong message? Why don't you just add instead of taking away? That's food for thought for delegates to General Convention.

If people are so hell-bent on a gender neutral service, then why can't you simply add one and call it Rite III. Why do you have to take away the ability to have a traditional service with older language? Why is it always all or nothing for our church? Just add it without taking anything away. Everybody needs to stop being so insistent on changing everything so as not to offend anyone. And when you do that, you end up offending tons of people that you didn't think you would offend in the first place! Just add; don't take away. When you take away, you are offending all the people that like the old way and saying that they are wrong and that they have to change or leave. Stop it.

Let's go back to the question. If we add it, will it bring new people in, and if we take it away, will it make people leave? Taking things away that are in the current prayer book will make people leave. Adding things without changing what is currently there so that both sides can have what they want is a much more logical and much more inclusive way of solving the problem. We say we are *inclusive* and yet we don't care if we offend somebody to change something to make it more inclusive in our minds. Maybe inclusive means both ways are great. Inclusive should mean that we're not going to offend people and say that their way of worship is wrong. Yet that is exactly what the Church does on a regular basis because they think they're always right.

I really don't mean to be rude and I don't want to come across as being negative, but the National Church is truly tone deaf and they need to stop and listen once in a while. I am appealing to every bishop and every person that serves as a delegate to any level of our church. Ask the question: will this decision gain members or lose members?

CHAPTER 14

Hope for the Future

I do have hope for the future of the Episcopal Church and of mainline Protestant denominations. They are an integral part of who we are as Americans. They are not just our glorious past; they can be our glorious future. If we are to preserve this institution, and if indeed it is worthy of preservation, then we need to act now. We first need to stop apologizing for who we were and who we are and embrace our identity. We need to stop pretending the decline will go away on its own by ignoring it or avoiding it. Only we, the members of the Episcopal Church, can save the Episcopal Church.

I see the Episcopal Church able to turn around the numbers and the narrative. We simply have to stop the bleeding and the headline will read, *Episcopal Church Stabilizes for the First Time in Half a Century.* If we start growing, even by a modest amount like five or ten thousand a year, we will be the *comeback kid.* If we can turn it around, then so will the Methodists, Presbyterians, and other mainline churches. Changing the numbers changes the narrative, so let's get started!

This is how easy it can be, if we break it down. If we have over 6,500 churches and if our average yearly loss is around 40,000, then each church is responsible for gaining six more members per year than they currently do. That will counter the losses by death or from people leaving. Six members per year per church will turn this ship around. Can you commit to doing that at your parish? If that is the only thing you made as your goal this year at your annual meeting and you put all you can into the effort, could you do it? *Yes!* In fact, I bet you could do even better.

This means you have to turn your focus to growth. I am saying all growth, not just growth of people who think exactly like you. Welcome all people to the church. This means you have to stop bickering and always insisting your way is right. Just breathe, relax, and grow. You must charge each commission with growing within your parish, and you should use the first fifteen minutes of every meeting and gathering to talk about how the decisions you make at that meeting can grow the church.

There is a lot we have not talked about. We did not talk about Episcopal schools. Preschool, elementary, high schools, or colleges are all key to the success of the Church. Those all need to be looked at and renewed with vigor. We need to plant schools as a form of evangelism. We also did not talk about the seminaries and the need for more qualified and younger priests and deacons. But these are discussions for another day or the next book.

I once saw a cartoon that showed the Roman Catholic Church saying, "The one true church," and the Lutheran Church saying, "The one true church," and the Episcopal Church saying, "The Episcopal Church." I like that. Let's be more like that! We don't need to make our denomination into *the one true church.*

Now I know that many will say Jesus was not concerned about numbers. I know that many will say that numbers for the sake of numbers misses the gospel and misses the point. And they are correct. But if we don't take charge of the numbers, we are dead. We are talking about an earthly institution, so in order to preserve and grow it, we need to be realistic and use earthly resources. Maybe God sent Moses and the Israelites manna from heaven when they were in the desert, but I doubt he is going to fix the roof or pay the electric bill for your parish. God helps those who help themselves, so we have to help ourselves to grow.

All of our talk is about downsizing, preparing for less members, having clergy who work a secular job part-time to supplement their income. It's all about selling rectories or properties, including 815 in New York—our own headquarters. We make excuses for losses; we accept it as reality. Downsize, restructure, become a mission are the words. Guess what? We won't need to do *any* of that if we just *grow!*

Stop the message of being membership losers and accepting that we are membership losers. Focus on growing to fill the churches so we can pay the priest and pay the bills and then do greater outreach. Change the dialogue!

I want to see sermons about growth across the nation's churches that don't skirt around the issue but come directly out and speak it. Say what you mean to say and don't cloak it in a story or in the spiritual. It is in the world, not out of the world, so please be as plain spoken as you can.

Many may not agree with my take on the church. Some may call it wrong thinking, not in line with the Bible, not what Jesus would do, and maybe even worse. Honestly, I don't care what some may think or write about this book. I am speaking truth as I see it. I want the church to not just survive but grow and change the world.

Let's try it this way as I have outlined for a few years and see if it bears fruit. Five years and it can be done. Five years for a church to turn around, if you follow the framework I have laid out and if you follow the spirit of what this book is about. Try it. We can't do any worse than we are currently doing!

I have stayed away from being overly religious in this book. Part of it is because of my own struggle with faith. I don't always know what I believe. Do I believe in God? Yes. Do I believe in Jesus Christ's teachings? Yes. I know that much. The rest sometimes confuses and confounds me. But the Episcopal Church is a place that lets me find my way at my pace with scripture, tradition, and, the most important, reason.

I want to end with something from the service of Compline. This is my favorite service in the prayer book. We used an older version with older language which was beautiful. When I was growing up I would go to our Christ Church choir camp called Camp Ogontz in New Hampshire and we would sing this at the end of the day. It brought me peace and it still does. Maybe it will for you, too. I feel as though the church is in darkness and this gives me hope for light.

"Before the ending of the day, Creator of the world we pray that, with thy wonted favor, thou wouldst be our guard and keeper now. From all ill dreams defend our sight, from fears and terrors of the night; withhold from us our ghostly foe, that spot of sin we may not know. O Father, that we ask be done, through Jesus Christ, thine only Son, who, with the Holy Ghost and thee, doth live and reign eternally. Amen."

Finally, I leave you with this: "Lord, grant us Thy light, that being rid of the darkness of our hearts, we may come to the true Light, which is Christ."

Now, as my former rector, Fr. Bob Anthony, would say, "Keep the faith, and spread it a little!"

CHAPTER 15

Growth Is the Focus

*Y*ou write this one!

About the Author

Caswell Cooke Jr is an elected member of the Westerly, RI Town Council where he has served from 2002 until 2014 as a Republican and from 2018 until present as an Independent. He was elected to serve as an Alternate Delegate for John McCain's two Presidential races and served as Vice-Chair of his 2008 Campaign for President in Rhode Island. Cooke was also an Alternate Delegate for John Kasich in 2016.

Caswell is a former radio and TV host who has interviewed countless personalities on the long running "Caswell Cooke Show" which featured guests including Conan O'Brien, The Beach Boys, Rev. Jesse Jackson, Senator Ted Kennedy, Dan Rather, Donny Osmond, Gov. Jeb Bush and former Vice President Dan Quayle among many other notables.

Caswell has booked and managed various musicians, most notably the 1960's British Pop Duo Chad and Jeremy, with whom he

Directed and Produced a documentary called "Yesterday's Back." He also Directed and Produced an award winning documentary titled "Mostly Music: The Journey of The Chorus of Westerly"

In the Episcopal Church, Caswell was a member of the Choir of Christ Church during his childhood and serves as Junior Warden of his parish, Acolyte Warden, Delegate to Diocesan Convention and head of the Communications Committee. He is passionate about the growth and future of the Episcopal Church.

Caswell lives in Westerly, RI with his wife Christine, his two daughters Maddy and Leah and his step-son Louis.

CPSIA information can be obtained
at www.ICGtesting.com
Printed in the USA
BVHW060515150821
614421BV00004B/90

9 781645 696384